I0463176

CLOSED DEAL
[The Focus Negotiator]

BY

Joshua Odogwu

Table of content

Book 1

Book 2

Book 2

GUTFUL NEGOTIATION
(Business Market Story)

This story was received from the business rulers. It is about an experience they had with some business intruders. You have the rules in another chapter of this book. Business rule will serve as perfection to the questions, intentional lapses pardoned in the story you are about to read.

Amazingly, things happen because something happens. All needs have what is called guts. The world of dealings has all the while been a kind of notches; some make it and make it well; and others fail and fail well. But if we must do it well, gi

ving the required is worth doing. Nothing ever is without negotiating.

Negotiation is like a syndrome, which must be propelled by guts, always in the rooms of the unusual, just like a dribbler with a target, working within or using what is available to get what is needed and to the target. They work on plans, they manipulate plans, and always have plans working on whether they orchestrate it or not, to the favour of their target.

But, wait a minute. Contrary to what we do occasionally, I have not seen the reason sufficient enough for anyone to spend above budget if perfect plans were made? And, from another point of view not getting all you want to get; why? I think this is simple. You either never budgeted; you had all available for use. Or you don't know how to negotiate. One of these is the problem.

The things I want you to start this phase with are firstly – there are incredible differences between utilizing an opportunity and working in plan. We work in plan. We do not change plan. Because our plans are perfect enough for our success; maybe the reason is that we are negotiators. In most sales I made there were flops, so slanted that it cannot wedge-up a falling slab. There were too-many-to count people who were sold by simply psyching them to understand the value of opportunity – sales technique.

The value of opportunity as a sales technique will always work because everybody everywhere is busy looking for the term "the right opportunity", a mindset imbedded in the executing port of the plan. Therefore people can easily, and quickly, are pulled when you create this minded-value, a period when you attract their heart and wholeness to listen to what you say/need them to do –this time, collaborate the pains of missing an opportunity with the satisfaction in getting what one wants; drive it towards getting them to do what you want.

But opportunity in the real look at it has no useful value except it rightly falls into plan –this is how you tell an opportunity. It is simply and technically utilizing better advantages, maybe using one nest to catch fifteen or more birds. Every alternation of course is not conducive, sufficient to your favour if you are not the one pulling, the one posing the chance.

Does opportunity come, or occur without any work done? No! It has always been a plan, so it should always be there when and as you want it.

Advantages are guest to excellent target –target with adequate preparation. Some of those my clients bought from me out of sympathies bonds created. Though they need what I could orchestrate my services to serve them, but they do not really have the plan to do so then. They had feelings[1] that made them to succumb when I came, which I mostly, am grateful. Prepared people don't look for opportunity. It comes to them because they have the opportunity –like terms attract.

Secondly before we start, learn to put ego aside when it is business time. Ego has a way of relating with crowds of asinine that compels people into regret-able and un-decide-able proposal. Ego has its place. This is powerful – when an intimidation is denying one what one could have. But when we know a need, nothing stops us, not even impressions.

Let us consider you as an instance. Have you walked into a superstore, and somehow you felt intimidated by the levels of things, especially the price, standard or the transacting? And so, seeing the systems, things going, the gut to play the game falls to sleep inside personality conscious, you defaced. Most, hear from within "don't be different!"You hear it like a whisper. These things happen either because of pride, silliness, or inferior feelings.

If you continue like this, then you cannot move a pace. Gut(s) is a daily required recipe for everyone that has a day; in-spite how the day looks like.

One lesson you mustn't just know but work with in negotiation is this: "learn to work within your bracket"; if where you find yourself isn't in range, try to fix it into the range, and if not possible, there could be a next –the next to meet could be in range and if not possible let it waggle if you have a time. You will appreciate this if you understand how people inflate standard simply maybe because they see you or they seem to the only one with such necessity.

You lose standard/control when you dance according to the beat. People of influence are people who lead dance; therefore be leader in whatever you are involved with. It takes guts to push to the best.

What you see out there before you are lines drawn by people like you; if you have made your target, you are not being serious violating your target because of intrigues. An attribute of adept negotiators is the extras they explore to get what they have tagged, even if it means crossing the opponent's line. Their bottom line is getting the deal within the bracket [total required to get a target].

And because we plan the deal, we keep the deal within, by doing everything possible. Time is something we can plug-on or plug-off depending on what we fully understand. If you care just reason with: I have my line(s), and you have your line(s); so why would anyone think I should break my lines for another's appeal, while some potato chips are thrown out so I can catch if I care to.

However, you must be ready as a negotiator to silence pride, silliness, and inferior feelings in your living; hold intrigue in a bottle sealed behind. This will help you push your target. We don't belong to the class who just spend because we have it to spend or maybe that is what the standard of the place is. We spend, understanding the propinquities of such action to our target and budget.

We spend because it is expedient. Remember what a negotiator said, "anything negotiated and fixed can still be re-negotiated"; you never can tell what may happen. It is all about doing what is neither normal nor ever done, exceeding the line, breaking the law of impossibilities: that is going the extra-ordinaries. Dancing according to the beat or sounding our beat is not main problem. It is doing what we do profitably and according to our plan(s).

There is only one-way to either beat down standard e.g. price –keep on negotiating firmly with the two sides of distributions [supplier and consumer]. Surround your guts with skills[2] so that it can always give the value it is expected to give.

---

[2] Negotiation ply and gambit

When you are embroiled with the right attitude [being positive] over a thing, you can always see that you can always develop and strategize your skill. So most times things don't work out the way we want, because we don't develop, we are always usual in thinking, known with a colour[3], doing the same systematic job spell [function]; simply because we don't have the required skilled-gut to develop our value.

The global organization is growing in a trend where systematic operational approach may deface; only people who have the guts to develop and reach-out can be promoted into helms[4]. Since organizations count per value, every asset must have its value on proportional line scaled in the firm. If job function must remain in its systematic/automated procedure, then robots are better staffs to use than human.

Humans are because they are developers with guts. They think: we (people) are... because we can think-out the expected solution. You are paid to use intelligence; that is the essence of your qualification. Use your initiative to create and implore solution. Don't use it for nothing valueless and unprofitable.

We would not de-emphasize the essence of bracketing[5] in negotiation. It takes wild[6] gut to circle out our bracket, so

---

[3] Styles and design
[4] Grow to the height attainable
[5] Marking a limit
[6] Experienced, and brave

that when you spend or initiate forum it must align your bracket. Bracket creates drizzling enterprise, babbling rooms; so therefore there is a how you do it.

Gut is the only power to the unknown, approaching the invisible, the impossible, and the like-un-attainable. You never can tell, a dollar per unit share could mean a lot millions in a bulk share purchase.

Maybe you go to brokers, they tell you the percentage price per deal; however it sounds you shell in for whatever reason. Maybe it is not negotiable. The earth has no license, and not even intimidation can license it except God. Only gut push us to break into boundary, which we all have been given the license to breakthrough.

Even when you try to see if anything better can happen at least, a little nibble, your waves could not forceful enough to drive an object into the broker. The most you could ever do in your dealings is to conclusively be induced into believing the trend is like that, never changed. This should be your motivation to negotiate: *if the earth turns, then everything in it can change, even things tagged "fixed"*. After all nobody was tagged history maker. We tag ourselves.

However a standard is postured, it was made by entities; and it is still subject to alteration by an adept negotiating entity.

Evaluating stock [share-holding] offers, both public and private shouldn't any longer be a kind of imposition. We need the evaluating factor; we have to own decision partly. The most concerned is the private placement. Don't you agree with me? Been $25.00 per share last time offer, and now new offer is $95.00 per same share is not sufficing again. Don't say "this is crazy"; we should not accommodate intrigues again. All markets are subject to negotiation.

Fluctuation may exist as a term[7] in the market but isn't there control? What are the factors that bring fluctuation, and how are these made? How can you tell me that the $50,000,000 I gave you to trade has depreciated with 45% loss? What jargon is fluctuation and depreciation to my business? For your business, you can be a nut. Stunt negotiation sounds stupid but always works better than some [refiners fire][8] –refining those blunts that can help be the loser.

You want us be part funding in your company indirectly or directly? That is no problem. We've being in it and might be willing to go with your proposal. But everything has to be justified and equitable. We understand our relevance in your offer and the relevance on our side, as well as the opportune-able pros and cons. But this has to be a good deal, don't you think? Give us what is possible,

---

[7] Normal and expectable occurrence
[8] Market union authorities and their policy

because we know what we want –appreciation of [OUR] value.

> Show your skill and competence by averting loss. A special thing you must know about entrepreneurs is that they plan risk but would never expect to lose.

How about the way the bankers, the governments, the realtors, the brokers associates, the supermarkets, the port-folio(s) leaders with their entourages and oligopoly[9] of enticement parade our intense[10]. When you see them what you see seem like pinnacle of standard, well knitted Italian suit, knotted-up with tie, looking like they are more gorgeous than faithful and guiltless angels on their glinting shoe. Their voice, echoing like satisfied authority that needs no thing. The phonetic accent alone is shackling. And you know how this can bruise one's feet, and with intimidation cramp ego of the target.

All these are out before you, looking un-approach-able like sea-centered loathing sculpture, as if you are not the cause for their either enthronement or survival. Sky-out of their circle let us see if they won't run after you, even with spent-life-to-build diplomatic proposal; begging for your brave deal, and hard earned wealth of opinion.

---

[9] Government, systems
[10] Powerful proposal, ultra-modern business acumen

Don't you see how the bash of newly arrived and ready brand hits market? I want you to imbibe the nature of gut; we all need ourselves to do business.

Or do you think pharaoh[11] was as foolish as that refusing them go? He knew that even the slavish Israelites are of great value. Human assets are invaluable. But you don't need to go the way it seems if you must be the pharaoh – the holder of power in his time.

The common/simple interest is value: <u>they either make you not to see your value or frightening you with theirs.</u> We all know the lyrics: believe in yourself, be confident, diligent, positive minded knowledge and more. These are boding pull in gut like inferred, but can't be without working it. You have to know yourself, believe in yourself [dream] and sell yourself [don't leave the dream in dream realm].

ABOUT BUSINESS (S)

Business(s) is a class of specie that nothing takes unaware. Even when they are making their underground works, passers-by hardly notice them. Only who has lived amongst them can identify the business symbols and maybe suggest what could be going on in the business clan.

---

[11] King of Egypt when God sent Moses [Exodus –Bible book]

My host characteristically is well known for something: they are imbue with irresistible infesting germ, if you let them be, they will not only spoil you by eating and getting you saturated with spooks and lousiness; and then they will convert you, making you more useful to their objective. You know that.

That is the negotiators initiative, inaugurated to make you re-value your stand, speaking to your intuition to do something drastically, and either garnish with more benefit, all on reducing your quote or you looses your chance -value.

But Adept Negotiators know how to see advantageous opportunity when people use activity rule on them: it is a simple conversion formula, it gives you the advantages to define their knowledge, know their weaknesses, and position for the best time[12] every dream always expect and at the right spot. It is a simple ideological formula: **regulate your time, wear their armour, but make out chance and slay[13] them knowing well the contra-goals.**

You allow them conclude they are using you so that you can control them; dreams work-out this time because that is what they need to inaugurate their dominance. It is unfortunate but quite typical the synonyms between world respected entities and terrorisms that escalated on the

---

[12]Without bent and free road, direct contact, to shoot into the goal-net
[13] Take as many as you can take from the market, and opponent

world trade center. Never think you are out, until you go to heaven. There is always a last man.

The lesson the world should have learned is that nobody who mother's the crowd, and not expect a feel of scheme, especially when encoded legality is held above ex-gratia (something that is morally right but legally wrong). Authorities in nationalisms are the breed of this.

When you meet business people and ask what is most important to them. The reply sure will be their business. They know the relevance of team, being like and keeping family in total one, working in united organization [vision].

The easiest way to either win or destabilize a purpose is to destroy their "house", and then even their pride, their force of unity, their glory [queen in business' kingdom] can be caught without being bitten. You know how protective they are about that pupa-like hidden figment. She is the glory, the pride and like the purpose. [Honestly, when this member of business' parliament said this, I did not quickly believe that the queen is also their purpose for eating wall and all they do].

She is the last anyone can see. Imagine the galleries and cantons of soldiers around her (a purpose). [The Member of Parliament did not give much concern to my grunt; maybe he knew I shall come to understand that point before he finishes]. Some of the things we hate are wandering and exposing our target. Business can relate to their business team; but anyone else sees it, even observant when we have got the goal.

I tell people that come to me for interview when they ask me some wrong questions, that I don't want marketers who have the mindset that marketers are wanderers, strolling along the street, wasting synergy without justifiable result, hoping to meet clients. I always like them to plan like business -people don't know when they do their works. They only fight to destroy what business has built. My concern is not about what/how many things you did. It is the result -giving me what I expect from you.

A plan gives directives and schedules. It tells more of who has target, I told to my one time market manager that every person that passes you by could be a posteriours potential client. Wandering keeps business without destination, without pride and without plan, just flouncing figure, and disturbing orderliness like slaves of time. But you can support them to achieve the goal I said to him

Sure, I will give the necessary support. And these classes of persons are the ones that come always to disturb you with stories of what they have done rather than the result. Deliverer only delivers without much talk. And story tellers talk much to impression you of their works – because results are speaking failure for them.

Two things make the speeches for people anywhere they are. It is either their activities [words of their mouth] or their benefits [results]. Therefore they would wish their activities: it [which is their works] should grant them your appeal.

But if you want to the control order [game], and then give them no direction –business(s).

> Business people often build their fort in secret, odd times, to them it is normal but to the normal it is abnormal, when nobody expects anything to be happening. It is keen knowing the propinquities between interest and perception, and distinguishing the uniqueness amongst both words. Conflict of these makes us wobble.

Sometimes, winning don[s] win when they choose to do those stupid things; it is all about knowing your interest, the environment concerned, and how to get it. People of bravo only wake up to see earth protrusion. Something is far going.

To be a winning negotiator you must learn to be readily definite. *Do your major negotiations when nobody suspects.* Portray disguised interest with its lodestar assured. You will start losing when you accept that you were taking unaware, and this makes a wrangler, struggling to cover the things you feel might be loopy holly on your part. Consenting to the standard is because you want to take charge.

And, when we [business] build our mountainous tent, there is no special thing that shows significantly this is the foundation, so ancestral, out-lived, the pillars of the house are never conspicuous, because nobody has shown it maybe. People can bring thoughtful fragments of the "house" but not the "how the house was built". Maybe the quality of what is used in the building that determines the firm strength of the team.

Outsiders can't, because we have in our discretion clandestine the source and pillars and foundations of the house. People have tried it many times, but rather than ruin, unknowingly to them we grow deeper and wider in the business. By this fact, the business family can't be cramped: you can crack down the walls and patterns but not our discretions, in this lies the secrets to the key.

Negotiating professions and successes is not all about I got it for A, and B, lost it for C, and tried but not good enough for D. Even though likeliness is, but the discretional ability to thrive over stubs is major key factor. Ask Robert Kiyosaki about the most important interest in success stories[14]: it is the discreet ability in crossing over times. Not luck. It is ability. Abilities hubs in keen

---

[14] Book by Robert kiyosaki

The power of the glory is not in how much you tried; but did you get it. If you lose at the end, it means you lost at the beginning: no winning plans, no winning survey, selection; or you have disguised loses. What is the implication? Getting it right the first time is adept and best, and possible. Gut will do its work of stimulation but being psyched up doesn't mean right wrench. What is then the deal? Gut adds to right ideal [strategies].

THE ROAD OF EXPERIENCE

It was a wonderful strolling moment one morning, you know: young zealous entrepreneur looking out for discovering(s) that can empower skills around us. I was walking through a borough one day; and that was because of how good the road was. I liked taking that route.

There was one of those earth protrusion where I habitually enjoy sitting to rest, refresh myself; do one or two things [side fun] before continuing to the farm. But some days later as I was doing normal hobby, I found out it was business home, something I dreaded most because of its bite, I never wished to have any form of closeness to that community. This was how it began.

I grew to know business as "soldier ants". And, if they attack you, the after-blight and discomfort automatically instills fear for business; so from that day I experienced [that bite] I chose not to be a scapegoat again, business public figure of triumph.

The truth of such decision is that, it has always been much uneasy and difficult adapting, changing pleasure-like habit that brings comfort. But because I don't want to be either ridiculed or retreat home without my goal, I stopped that rest on the protruded earth.

Bob, see! Business house is such a horrible, one-of-those wonders of the earth. Their harmful ability is so insignificant in such a way that innocent soul may fall victim. Only the man who had encountered them can tell what soldier ants can do: you dare not look for business trouble. You will either have to spoil the deal or they drain you.

Now as business, we always have one goal, one purpose, and one rail of road; the forces and composition of our synergy is always reserved. So if you must be troublesome, heraldic with sprouting veins then, stand on the way of the agenda. This is if you know it. Every time you see them moving to & fro their rail what are they doing? We are servants you know, carrying out a mission we have been sanctioned not to allow any interruption.

I think my friend that, Business as negotiator is perfectly suit for negotiators of all class to learn, especially their rules. I learnt about a man who learnt an inscription "don't OK the first offer," so because of that, at gunpoint, his life was at stake, he had the nerves to negotiate his life with gun. The robber only clamped and the inexperienced negotiator calmed down and allowed the robber with is demand; while he felt so bad loosing, and even blaming the instructor.

When you lack the right thing, you do the wrong thing. The law of necessity was not on seat that day. Define necessity always. Do what is necessary, and let go what can't change a fact.

Knowing this law knows how to always make a deal with both sides going home satisfied and winning. A basic fact about my negotiator "business" is this: you can't tell the foundation of the wall [house -what is making the team a bond] and you can't know their agenda until you see them singing home with it.

I can only help you spot their motivation but can't tell you the "how". Their agenda is their foundation, what made them a community. I can only help you spot their motivation [the essentials], but can't tell you the "how" now. Their agenda is their foundation.

> We build walls to cover our course. Yes anybody can crack the wall and destroy it but I assure you, not the agenda. And this is what some negotiators do: good when it comes to cracking walls than taking hostage the agenda. And when they do these irrelevant jobs, which could uncover their

plot, they ignorantly project egos of the triumphant.

Consider this: cracking the walls brings challenges, takes more time, and makes it more cumbersome. Why not leave walls mimic standing while you have found your way in.

And also, when you arrest the agenda you have the people under control. So simple and easy, but work it out and tell me what it cost. Idiots are always idiot, but still they have and know what they call secret and how they keep this secret.

Most smart business personnel and dealers, what they do in every transaction are to firstly calculate and checkmate the key to the deal, waiting for any action from you. This is often considered when you are almost near to the verge of losing. Just flash back to the man and the gun: no intelligent dealer would either give chances or allow concessions worth more than the profit; yet so many in their orbits of stimulation have given out what they should not have given, and the other guy will simply collect it as a first bonus offer.

Concessions that should have stood you a chance of gaining an advantage is taking advantages from you. And you know this is how we lost some deal –because of what we have conceded to the other opponent. So, we stand at a point where we consider instead of losing it all let's just get something out of the deal. Be informed that there is always the key to every target that puts the target at your command/service.

As interestingly situational as the case of the man and the gun is concerned above, the key to what the robber want is the life of the checkmated man. The robber got the right thing. He would be stupid and goalless if he had accepted the fifty over fifty offers by the key-point. And the man is not a too good negotiator because he tried to beat down demand that can take his life. *-don't expect an opponent to be acting stupidly until you pilot stupidity in them.*

In cases like this, what do we do? Taking the law of necessity, calmly save the life [which is the supposed to be the target of the man before the robber], protect and open rooms for the goal even if it means giving up something. Let go the wallet without losing everything!

However we would look at it, there is no way the wallet could be his target. His target is money, but he believes you put money into wallet. So it is one thing that the robber wants a thing but doesn't really know the key to his satisfaction. And fidgeting would have simply helped the notice requester know the right point to ask.

I believe whatever is the content of the wallet is only means to trivia, but the man himself could own billions. This is not what the business people do as trained pioneers: you must learn never to break the first of the rules, because it is like a cringe to all the rules. They do this and also, machinate when called for –it is all necessity.

I had to change walking side even though I could see the business building at a short distance. Coming back from [farm] I realized a confused movement: a treasure was already found under the business building, what I dread has cubic of fortune for miners; other animals have planned taking it again [yes again because they initially had it before business crushed them out of the market], and humans would not mind taken it –because of its usefulness to all the parties –a market is nobodies home, but we all want to lead the trend. Could that have been their foundation or maybe the purpose of their agenda?

> Let me share this secret with you: that treasure is the market you and I need, which the business building, signifies dominance. The business agenda is the key to that treasure. And their foundation must be discovered before the treasure can be taken away from business control.

However, in the animal world, conference was already held enviously about the business: "the wall is scary, they were [assumption] more powerful colossus than Gulliver to have caused such an earthy eruption", some of them were astounded enough to know how they build the wall and others felt business could be giant-like wild animals.

"So how can we relocate the business or possibly extirpate their bands from us and live satisfied."

VISIT YOUR COMMUNITY OF BUSINESS MARKET

These issues bug managements some times; especially in midst of competition when a brand seems to be dominating or taking from you, what you have spent life-years to build. Sometime, management fear how to go without spoiling chances or losing everything left. And others go by default. Risk is better than null. Well, you are in the game already –you need the solution to defeat competitions.

As powerful and skillful business are, you don't see the trace of power in them. But they are quite intelligent specie. So for the other animals to negotiate their resolution, a spy would have to be sent to the business kingdom because they [business] are the leading brand.

At the entrance, everywhere was calmed [incredible, unusual, and unexpected][15]. This impression stage is what you are always thrown into to delude your devices and probably leave you in awe of "what". And nobody was seen, it looks somehow an antique place. People ask themselves the question "how do I go from here"

---

[15] First impression, market experience

You ought to see the expansions of the hair pores on his skin –the hairs stood as strong as an iron for scares, very most terrified: "so my life ends like this, oh! Help me God", he said. Still gawk through the tunnel-like chamber, he moved in a bit, followed a branch, there he saw what he never believed he could see in a hole. He saw a tiny growing tree [there are always things that distract in the rails of negotiator, if you follow them, do like who they are].

This is a disguise, outsiders will see it as disorganized, an abandoned deal or better still, incapability. But you know the chains of plan –don't forget that good players scatter to win. [In as much as it is game ground, anything is expectable, every team have their codes and understanding, and applications]. He got nearer to the tree, climbed it and surveyed everywhere possible, and climbed down. He moved further into the heart of the solid oblique mud, still observing.

> Don't forget the lessons you need to learn quick enough, because of the impressions

After several diversions, it was obvious that the errand animal may not find his way out because of how dazzling and antique the home is –lifeless. While unknown to this spy, he has past many claws in which the business people hid themselves.

Guide yourself well with wise caution when you play game with experts. It may always seem normal, which will make inexperienced player play as if he is so valiant. Experts may not hurry a game, but their move, plot, and shoots quakes any challenge. [Could you believe other business people were observing the spy?] He was quite harmless, fearful, confused, going like he is searching for something. Truly he seems to be looking for something: the way home and what must be in the erupted earth -there is always a cause.

Business people with caution were expecting a time with the spy, when he will be void; that is, either sleeping out of tiredness or something alike. Remember every player always expect a time of no other stub.

> Always have it in mind -there is always the time when opponents exhaust strategies, or maybe need to rest. This is what they say, "the chips are down" so you can tear through and explore!

I don't understand! You mean as skillful as the business people are, they still look for weak points [opportunity]? Yes they do. You will come to know why. Maybe they were actually staging the spy until he exhausts all plan and synergy.

One of the riskier negotiations you can ever venture is to spy someone who is seeing you; who you know, know you are a spy with negative motive. [They play it like prank].

Or a negotiator who hardly utters a serious word [seems not to have any plan]. This guy though was in a disposed position, yet was muttering conglomerating attitude; a stranger, possibly an opponent rendering a reliable obedient.

[Negotiators don't look for trouble; they only try to play the right and best card]. Few hours later the spy got tired of groping and stooped calm. While he was having a mind glance over the experiences, without any tangible result, he slept. Strategic skill makes opponent tire easily. When you don't act when you are expected to act, you push them into goggle, question they can't be sure of the answer. Be sure of this: they will only make available what is within their reach.

In case you've forgotten the trio-negotiators[16]: this spy is only one amongst or supposed to be the intelligent or the informant negotiator. Now, the team would likely depend on him to sail through negotiation intrigues and perhaps provide them with what they need to win. The hope [knowledge] of success anchors on him.

As informant or intelligent negotiator, you must know your disguises and how to get your information necessary. You see that I am not surprise seeing him express such a reliable obedient. He has to; because the key of their victory begins with the information he would give to the entire team.

His sleep was natural. The body needed it. And these times come on organization, when it seems nothing is really happening. They fall to sleep. Everything in a kind of rolodex; the organization or an arm in an organization has gone to sleep; the neck of the target is hanging on a thousand feet tall gallour. The company needs breakthrough to the next stage.

> The question I would ask is this: how do you achieve a job more tedious and impossible than you thought? In the thick of the job, right in the enemy's territory; evidences are with you that you are not a good-intended spy. You want to take the market they have not decided to leave. And you are yet to get the most vital thing; you've not hit the target, only to be in a discomfiting situation?

While he was asleep one of the soldier ants intentionally came near and punched the spy with its tentacles, and speck hard at him. He jumped up with that inner gripping fear. You can call it frustration, or opposition that threatens the continuity of our advancing to the intended target –the fear that he has been caught; only to see a too little ant. He disdained the business ignorantly, warned the ant. And looking back, he said: "who are you?" Asking the business and "what are you doing here?"

This isthmus uttered no word but was showing a relevantly mutual interest. So he asked again. "Have you ever seen the merchantpersons of this clan?" "How about you tell me something: are they good and hospitable people to dwell with?" The business looked at him and wagged his head. Remember what I told you about people who confuse who you with impression yet, don't easily utter words.

In my negotiation theory, there are three kinds of speakers; two of these three are most crucial, and one not too crucial: those who don't easily utter words and those who pack dust with words. The attitude above of the spy is that of a sucker, attaché; a kind of psychology that positions you on a seat of dependant, infant, pamper-able, novice, deformed; speaking to the opponent to help you with anything that can be possible.

This kind of attitude works on [magnets], people who easily receive or accept [motions]. But, right in the business mind, a clue could be too much endangering to give away, confidential is meant to be kept. However too good, pleasant, beckon, and acceptable an offer is, don't be OK with it. You must jerk at it; you never can tell what will happen. Is it not absolutely siphoning and subtle how this spy spoke unsuspicious and pretentiously with the "business"?

However, the spy offered the business a concessive prize. And as I expected, the business took it and said "thank you for your kindness; I hope to see you again and probably be of better help to you. But now, sorry I am not in the right mood to help anybody; maybe next time." He walked out of sight and joined his neighbours in the clicks.

> Note that the language of concession implies in the other way round that there is a bigger thing I can get from you if you could take this little offer from me. It could be insinuated to be nodes to making things better.

This offers me the chance of making my point quite clear: concession is vital in deal; and if we must tangle, we must then concede. But the question is this how much is a concession helping your target? Remember that there is no concession without interest. And if it is observable that no risk no reward; without sowing there can't be reaping; why should we think it is cordially not prospective to offer fugitive appraisal?

Always attempt to give" fugitive appraisal"[17] to your challenges or forces pulling you against wish or into compromise. It knocks off intensities of motive, making you look connected and committed to another's good [so it seems]. The fact is that no fugitive gives worthy praise to the master of bondage.

---

[17] A Business negotiation gambit used to diffuse attacks or pressures before it is launched

The common lesson is this: don't be carried by people, carry them on psychotropic.

The spy had futile stroll. Sometimes after the encounter with the soldier, the intelligent negotiator returned back to his crew. Have in mind he took note of what he saw, ignorant made him still went home sad, and with a wrong opine for an answer. Sometimes thing don't always work the way we have experienced, or seen in prognostic realm; so that we can learn the strange part of occurrence.

This is a typical scenario: the men you negotiate with, there are direct and close approaches you take towards them and they get clues to what they shouldn't know. It is possible that anybody in the market could be a dealer who is just in the market to bid the business you've build with effort of years. So, treat all responsively as such as is necessary. And sometimes believe the vision/purpose only; and not necessarily the opponent's reaction.

The spy's goof put the business on complete security. This is a tide of habits –most of the referred stooges may not truly be that. They could be simply learning under experience. Business showed stunt stooge habit, while the spy was really showing that something was in the mind

Hope you never thought business [gutful and powerful] wouldn't look for that time every goal expect? Business were seriously looking and plotting the opportunity, because it takes this orchestrated kind of opportunity to

win and accord such appraisals. It is not the strength
[ability] but the concord. Contrary to this, leads waste
rather than conserving energy.

All are skills. Skill is all about how you can use what you
can get to get to what you need, which includes
opportunity maximizing. We create it, orchestrate it, and
prepare for it, and use it.

He returned back to the people, good enough no harm
[as they observed all over him]. "What did you see and
can we get to the treasure", I mean, how? The group of
the opponent asked the spy. [The chief's interest is always
on the goal].

"Well, [bent his mouth] the protruded earth", said the
intelligent negotiator, "is wonderful, and so many long
and short lane with nobody in irrelevant; "it was only one
stubborn brat, a little ant that came inside and squashed at
me. There were also, diversions and a spunky tree". The
situation couldn't be defined properly. This poor
definition is because one is a better negotiator than the
other; if not, opportunities are equal.

YOU'RE NOT THE ONLY NEGOTIATOR IN THE MARKET –BE CAREFUL

Can you tell why the little soldier ant refused to utter a
word as required by the spy? There is always the place

where courteous formality should be in business and when to allow policy rule. In deal there should be polite squash[18]. This squash is like severe chasten to purge off glows of feign that is projected, offered to you. Sometimes this things look like a surprise

This is what some do. They give you that room of formality, because they know that until you understand the familiarity, bosom-friend, teammate, you won't consider favourable decision, decisions bad enough to share your goal secrets, or even trade with them. So they offer you that room, such kind of close relationship – intentional friendship.

What you see that business do was policy uphold. You must be tactful, especially in response. Integrating between being a person of courtesy and a person of the policy of the organization, you may call it etiquette; or squash and tenderness is analytically ambidextrous. Why?

Whenever you are given a concessive prize, know that what is required of you is betrayal, perhaps you are about to sell your hide, your pride for a morsel of meal. Concession is an invariable vote-voce telling you to be more skilful; especially when you have not asked for it [concession]. This, the business knows. However it comes: wittingly, voraciously, or scarcely, be skillful.

---

[18] Criticize options

We mustn't mistake things. Adept negotiators are cosmetic: wrier, blather, their mute is an impression, expecting the best you can't further violate. They give words but not their key-word. And when they get the goal you would not have believed that is what they wanted, both in times of spying and times of execution. But one thing is sure; when it is time to shoot they don't hesitate to shoot –see the business rules. Somehow, the little soldier ant has been able to know what the spy want.

The spy's report intensified the intrigues in the mopes of the gigantic group. That spy was actual a minus to that team.

Now by the side where I stood, my greatest surprise was this: don't they understand themselves? Does it mean in animal world [world of diverse people wanting same thing] there is no locution trail? I mean it shouldn't be so anonymous to everyone there. Somebody should have the experience of business' attitude. Or maybe the spy is misconstrued.

However, we know business to be ventures that enjoy warmth atmospherics peculiarity, proficient at utilizing resources and stump and even other existence that services that same purpose; even though they seem so crispy. Could this be the reason why the animals are after them [may be business have eating their homes]? Or at least here lays weak point [crispy] to use against.

Until we seek to know, things may not be rightly done: even the giants have weak points. [They have attitudes of failures]. Knowing somewhat(s) about the business should be opts for business opponents to play on; but how have they goofed over! The problem is having target without proper amelioration and knowledge. They were consumed with knowing the secrets of the goal rather than their goal actualization.

> You may ask: isn't all the same effect? Yes, but the reality is that some steps are obstacle [obscurity] to other steps. When you go for your goal, you go to it; and not your opponent if they are not the goal. Opponents are obstacle to opponents. Remember, "When there are no suspects, everyone around the scene becomes a potential suspect that can lead to the point if followed in adept way."

Learn to choose the right choice amongst options. Weaknesses are the easiest way to winning a tough team. As in humans are fallibleness so also are his involvements. There should be a limping point around. You can't easily win strength. You can only win the weakening or the weak -this is your stout heart.

The animals want to know the secrets of their continuity and goal; because they are at the verge of death.

"You can't just be a destroyer, your presence terrifies other, and people wouldn't mind leaving the deal for you because they know they can't compete with you; causing a business volcanic eruption, which you enjoy and we suffer heart-prick". "We have continued to re-work on this you made waste. We have lost almost all possibilities yet you are still like the lord of the ring." These are what I heard some of their executives say at a stage. "Business is if you sell one day, and I sell for seven days it is fair-enough but this is not case. We are completely out" what an ironic riddance.

This is their grunt: business in pursuit of their goal has tampered with others treasure, their homes, and their choicest, made others loose potential client, and interrupting others from achieving their goal. What else makes a business profit if not customer?

The cloak of their [business] policy has naturally reformed to be skillful in getting the goal without breaking the rules; so business eat into things if necessary without considering how OK it feels with the opponent. But because of the way they eat through, you would not easily know until it's been eaten through. It irritates, and most, frustrates when you can't stop a destroyer. I understand.

Would we believe it is so possible for the business to have begun and finished a bough lump of wood? They must have been seen thin and fizzling, can't hurt, believed can't eat through no matter the effort, even seen to need help.

Don't ever believe your "opponent" is that weak, or maybe, needing a compromise-able helps in-spite how it looks. I mean the most wrong state of mind you should not daringly be as a negotiator is to assume the state of loosed-control –I am powerful. Anything goes, anything comes. Opponents are weak. I will trash them out with a wave of hand. I can always make-up things. Because, the subjective truth is that you can never be too powerful to need no help.

DON'T SIP BONE

Negotiation is all about the target. It is not sorely how it plays; it is not your duty to help your opponent get some winning or. It is his to get what he wants, that is why you have an opposing [contra-] negotiation; although, anybody can entertain if they have it in the crafty device.

One can play well without a formal target, indirectly becoming market-dog[19]; and you can play badly with an achieved target. But when you play well without achieving your target, the opponent will only pass a shadow cur[20] to you; impressions like "thank you very much, it was nice doing business with you, we look forward to having more better deals".

---

[19] Ready for anything thrown that comes the way, moves to and fro without any position
[20] Sort of mock

Why will they not look forward to having better business time with you, when they had a good time already with you, even call you back after long time? They will be gutful enough to tell you that, because you have always been so good, you helped them achieve their goal; you will be their best [favourite] client or contact when further deals come out. And you will be happy for the relations deceptive spices.

Is there anything wrong being helpful? No. But, it should not be at the detriment of your goal. Priority demands your goal first. When we define negotiation as being a game where you win and I win: we are only being logical and factual. It is not your duty to get bothered with this; because no negotiator looses it all. Your duty is to focus on your goal.

Let me hint you about a past. Before business got the place they occur presently, the same work-process this negative negotiators went and failed, business did and passed.

I am sure that when one of the business people strolled by, probably to spy the newly discovered prospective market; it was quite insignificant and unnecessary following after him, people did not observe him. Maybe he had feigned and disguised everything, either as a philanthropist; and they tell him "nice man welcome to the market", because they like such. Or he looked like a hopeless helpless survival, who they will like to use. Anything is possible for a negotiator.

Instincts vary. You know, the distinctions between my assessments about you and the reality of what you really are may likely be two different things. A Good judgment is base on reality.

However, the business passed through leaving a pretentiously insignificant "landmark" and took tidings home. They analyzed, re-organized, and re-sent a different business, which is the major negotiator, the executor with directly focused details.

He got there and stood, maybe before the tree or something else; made a tactical peel-off, and was pleased because the deal got a hedge to peel into the center of the market. Do you think it is so possible? Yes, it is, if you do the right job rightly. They firstly placed a landmark on which the second leaned on; it is like an exuding node.

If you examine closely, the second guy didn't bother to survey. Maybe because he has the isothermal details he should have got. But I think when you try to be too much careful you attract care-look. Let them not know your motive at least in the interim.

Don't let them read interest toward your key weapon and advantages. If they do; will not allow you get to the point you want –already you are in to cut an interest that could have added to them. They may see you later with your goal in your hand. Note: there is no duplicity in been tentatively informed and skillful.

>Bone is not what we sip, because it can harm us. It can only be chewed if we must eat it. Therefore be thorough, and do not give excuses for your responsibilities. This can occur when we feel not responsible.

PLY THE INSIGNIFICANT DIFFERENCE

So, when the deal was set, the business left the asterisked portion, and moved around to create activities for them; both those sneaking and peeping, and those carefree in the society. Can this be so effective? Maybe somebody almost caught his target. But leaving the asterisk point diffuses not only every plot, but has placed them in technically confused suspense.

When it was night [they are not coming back, maybe they were just buyers that came to the market], which for one reason or the other they left the scene [relinquish].

Having concluded their analyses and hopefully waited for a signifying action, or maybe when they have seen more implicative details than the common scrap on the surface, and nothing was forthcoming; it was then the business came back to that asterisked portion and worked into them.

It is not necessarily wise to despise little efforts or minor signals, because it can move mountain when you least believed. When it was morning the loosed-confidants returned and reviewed everything: things were as normal as yesterday; while somebody has been busy with his focus inside the <u>root of the visible [the market]</u>, gaining as many grounds as possible.

The things that are always visible in every market or environment are things especially, people with needs; you will always find a need in the market. And this is what negotiators look for in the first instant -where they enter through. That asterisked point symbolizes a need in the market. It was a contact the negotiator invigorated in the auspices of what discussion he had with the contact person or company. He could have gone there to buy something. He could have also gone there and just initiates an enthusing topic with them to find what he needs.

You see the power of activities? It placed them [opponent] on an indefinite suspension, perhaps doing something else, rather than competing rightly; until they finds a grace to know the reality. Whether or not the business was in a way dramatizing the fact that "all works without play makes jack a dull boy" I can't truly deny the effect. The evidence is that his principle of activities worked out for him, and more better for the entire goal.

Note: the activity scheme was with a group different from the one he made contact with, but all are in the same market.

Success is not in the size, it is in the wisdom of the application of your skill. Activities don't only pave way in for you but it allows you the lance to execute your plans as planned and, without any "opposition" or refuting. Challenges are hopeful, but if you do your "first things[21] first" orderliness, you will always have solutions to challenges.

No adept negotiator goes into a deal without first "knowing" the deal: those "who(s)" in the deal, and the "where(s)" about the deal, that is absolutely nitty-gritty of all the "knows" about the deal, so that in midst of challenges you won't be caught with a fish in your bag. Possibilities are that deadlocking could stand on but navigating successfully is most important. Business did because they know the rules and the right attitudes.

Like I thought, before the business must have asterisked the target, since he did survey everything around and on the spot, he knew what he needed to know, nooks and cranny, the exit point from deadlocking deal, the manipulating and influential part that concerned his asterisked, and the controlling decision.

_____

There are two major things every negotiator doesn't want around their gaming: deadlocking and, insatiableness.

There are some negotiators who have the scheme to create deadlocking to open way for their target, it is still the skill. The central fact here is that you don't want deadlocking to deadlock your target. So being inside the deal has no threat whatever of what is going on. He is just pushing, and pressing harder his target, cutting down tattling shadows with wholesome knowledge. You know you are more in control if you are inside. Being inside is having grounds, weight, control, connections of the business and market. It is not just having the name, the location [building] and all those self-connected parts we institute.

Meanwhile, as the business was progressively achieving his aim, the opponents were busy chasing air and musing; maybe, it's because they have different motive from the business(s), or their intelligent-quo is untrained.

Two days past, neither the business nor any change was seen. After a week, the agitated fellows re-planned a new agenda: activity has confused them. As a negotiator working on intelligent, be thorough, every act is suspect-able.

First reason, they couldn't imagine where the business was, they can't tell what really happened, what they were following finally seem to be miss-of-lode or fear of lost.

How? They never believed the business could have entered; probably there wasn't any grazing or grunting; or narrowed and conspicuous hole as a sign that something is inside working. It is a "dumb skill" in negotiation where the working silence is more promising than the vaguer audience. The other reason is that they don't know how to protect their interest.

And regarding dumb skill: don't expect an adept opponent to give you a threatening signal. When it happens be sure someone is not about falling into trap(s).

In Negotiation anything is necessary but, we look at the insignificant differences critically; because that carries the adept moves. The sure seen most time spreads dust.

Don't under-size the mouth of a needle because of the gigantic size of an elephant. Scientism has proven with the elastic law of expansion, explaining that if things can expand, then smaller object can contain or accommodate bigger objects.

Negotiators have always lost the deal unknowingly because of this adept move by the adept negotiator: things so minor and irrelevantly placed as though it means nothing could be their eyes. And because they don't want you see it; they just shade it up, you think it is the custom, maybe they are blind or having eye deformity. Negotiators shade-off your eyes[i].

Fine! That is what he, she, or they need you to believe so you can work with. I only know it is the way of the dealers prank; but even if it is the custom, insist on seeing it. Fix your hand if possible into the eye- focus on it; and dig through it. I remember an old neighbour, who was studying law. Many of the times we have caught him pretend to have this deformity –wrong eye set –we call it [half past four (4) eye]. When they look at you, you won't know, you will think they are looking somewhere rather. A target carrier has no other friend except target.

DEADLOCK IS NO END

Impediments and deadlocks are not always final conclusion on your target. These might be means: that is, sniffing points to exit. But deals don't end like that. I am sure there is a solution you aren't seeing yet, because you have confined your pros, your eyes are not yet fixed to the unknown, perhaps breaking through the limits, the boundary an opponent, or challenge has threatened your gut. *Negotiation becomes so interesting at points of intrigue, when disadvantages start to speak.*

Have you in a negotiation, after refusing trying to ensure your stand is firmly defined, encountered when your opponent, though did not buy your proposal, but has an alternative, and is willing to offer you every make-possible incentive if only you allow the way. In-spite how openings are, it impedes something.

I tell you my story: I accept concessions but on the basic reason that it is a plus, not to allow you use me to achieve your aim. Concessions rather, enable me to think smarter because I already know it is not free. Everyone working do it just to derive satisfaction, either affecting the environments or boosting their standard.

Reciprocity should define our union. What are the contra-values? Most of us know CEOs, MDs and management decision moves at times. Sometimes, it looks like devaluation and sometimes it sounds like promotion, whether there are reasons or not for it. And some of us when we see these claws of contracts, deals, and promotions hanging us back, keeping us busy, we tend not to think about necessity- target, ignoring the big fish because of the little crayfish, or the allusive image of a bigger and easier to get fish.

The truth is that you understand it more living it. If it is true that the same thing it takes to grab five gram is the same thing it takes to mold five million, then why won't you synergize and mold your buck? The place of utility is misplaced if we rather prefer saving the seed to sowing it, because it may rot away and we lose everything.

I had plans of better global community, giving room to the village of globalization. The aspiration, life-targets, call it business plots were booming in both my files and mind, efforts were on the grounds of establishment; that was when the company I worked with realized my value –my status was overdue promotion. I don't just know how, whether it was natural trail or through planted information for such spontaneous realization with alacrity. Things happened in ways that were dramatic.

There are so many things that happened around this but, I was promoted with triple-rate increase in my earnings, first I was made the warehouse manager, and secondly, General Manager; managing another man's business when it was never my root, like accountants who are so busy counting other people's money. This is good if that is the life you signed, but if not, for how long? In-fact, wisdom demands that in times like this operate on business rules beginning the first: rules of necessity- utilize the concessions and achieve your goal.

Note: this is a practical scenario, the company may not have the intention of killing your dreams and sometimes some do. But this is the ware-fullness- don't be manipulated and don't be persuaded to bench your best player, or skip the reality of what you have dreamt especially in the nick of time of and in the dream.

> Concession is good in motivating result-full people, but it has a way of keeping you within its devices. Your ability to define and work with priority is a symptom of maturity in a course.

YOU CAN TURN THE CLOCK'S HAND OR STOP IT

Business rules are dynamites when it comes to negotiation: you are always in control and never out of course. You can understand how the opponents were placed in an indefinite suspension from their goal, even though yet to realize it. And in most occasions you have to get Actifed or any other preferable ache reliever to relief you of the aches acquired from those pressures of activities.

A special thing about the rule of activity is that when it works on you cannot easily know. It is like normal business, normal opinion that sounds appealing. I have seen someone pushing "activity" to some other persons like a "proposal". Looking at it, you will hardly call it game. It looked so decent and impressive. You can imagine how that could have worked on the "old market leaders", people who "business" took over from?

The worst people to deal with are those classes who seem to show interest and yet are silent. You can't see any sign of further action. They would not only help in spending your time but they will keep you busy groping and hallucinating without doing other important things. Not that they don't know what to say, just that it is not time; maybe like what we know about intelligent negotiator[22]. They don't give suggestion to a stranger, [to] someone who is not a team; so they regulate you to be under their plan. I know the reason why they don't do this is because suggestions [communication] create relationship, and this leads to contact, reflection, and knowledge.

What would you do when you find yourself under a web of activity?

You may not be too smart if you deadlock the deal, though it can be a way but, the pros and the cons are part deciding factor. My advice for you till you find yourself in such scheme are firstly, build up in-despicable value in and around yourself. Don't be on the losing or needing side and think of deadlocking. Sometimes you could be a patient dog with schemed strategize target. And you can also borrow a value and sell to them if you don't have any good enough for such a client of combat. Lastly, if you have no good value, or not at all at stake then shun the deal for the man who must loose. He comes back with a reviewed and reformed plan.

While the gloom of intrigue webbed on, the business never seemed to show up again. Time wasn't either remedying the situation. To your "tent oh Israel" was the last gospel. This makes us understand that in game one loose advantage(s) and another gains advantage(s). It depends on what and how you're crafting.

Business wasn't loosing time advantage. Only the opponent who I can say was been played, were losing time. Several Weeks later about thirteen or fourteen weeks, people notice protrusion of the earth. What awe! "You mean something really went on, even though we were constantly up on watch?"One of them said. Somebody was busy working out objectives, while the others were busy following steps with assumptions lousily. There were subject to outcome. If you must play rightly and timely to stop an opponent, learn to crack every nut. Do not always wait for an outcome.

> This is what happens to us when we lose. The truth is that we don't want to lose and also, our loosing is not because we could not have won; but we allow frail[23] on the sits of decision.

Yes, the way we have seen ourselves loose at times baffles! In-spite the best we did. The fact is that winning is internal[24]. You don't give chances if you must win. The best you can do when you are on winning row is to do everything doable in the extra-ways. Risk has always been there, and in some unfortunate incident savaged dreams; but there are also and always the right times when we do manage the risks -you manage risk by undertaking the risk.

I see it abruptly unreasonable to believe there wasn't at least one micro-organism that can lead in the sanitization of the walls. It is just that the power of hallucination did

---

23 outcome, what happens
24 Mind information and frame

not see the vision so the people perished. When you always depend on sensible opinions, credible facts, and opportunistic gland[25], you may not know that most wise and good fortune take the shape of nonsense. Call it luck or risk, the underlying point is that you have to go the extra ways to give nonsense a sense, an unproven opinion[26] a try; and so you caught the right and big fish.

How can be this done? Simple, if you know how to read a mood, and interpret a signal you can read the target trend.

Look at the marketers and branders, how do they go about it? They all have most nearly the same motive: be the leading brand, get the customers, make more profit and satisfaction, and dominate the market. But see how nonsense makes sense. You don't follow trend to be a trend; you make and project your brand to be a trend. Majority of the sustaining class of business research every others and come out with what we call UNIQUE in all ramifications.

Every brand has its market and scheme. Mobile Telecommunication Network [MTN] Company in Nigeria for instance, is soaring in its lines of attraction. What we had [Nitel] before this emergence leads to snoring, a very deep sleep, but when this came into the same business we felt not only a great relief, but communication was revived brought to life. It has taken

---

25 Appealing choices, available offers
26 Been sure the asterisk point is not a deceptive port, impression

the shape of brand, becoming a trend. It has been known with a word somehow; don't speak the same except you are MTN promoter or delusive competitor that pranks denigrate[27]. Build your system and confine it enough to enable the market adapt to it. This is all you need to do – making the market adapt to it. Once this is done, your work as a brander is just pedaling the business.

Market lawmakers believe that every product and brand has its entity and its market, so they work on need and keen interest to give all satisfaction. Your brand loses its integrity when you are a confused brand. The market's eyes of instinct sees, so they'll leave you since you are leading them to nowhere –you are not worth to be the leader. Same thing they do is what you do, therefore since you have no vision those who have objective wouldn't want to compromise any chance flouncing. Negotiate your brand, your business to the position you want to be and let the market see it the way you want it seen. The story I am narrating still has more to how this can be achieved.

Have a word, a tenacious vision even though life is much subject to influence, but you'll see interest. If you must achieve your target you must first give the market a target –target of the "most frequently come back". Play to the top from the bottom [available contact].

---

[27] Fugitive appraisal

IMPROVISE CONTROL

In a nutshell, in negotiation business there are so many signals and different antennas, some of which might be clear. But it is expedient to initiate that getting the real signal tells much of the people who know what they want and do it. You are not in the game to keep yourself busy or perhaps in customary shadow –public or market entertainer while market business is on. You are in to get a tangible boost –magnanimity, maybe getting the major interest. Therefore find the signal that is eager for your word, and start business with it.

Sellers know how to sell what they have to sell and buyers know how to buy what they want to buy; negotiators are not just either creators, but are unionist. They make the business, keep the business and they succeed the business just like the business. And, sometimes people don't know how they are working it out until after game if there is such capable grace.

Did I tell you that every Perfect and competent negotiator's team has the three functioning attributes[28] of negotiations? The team ascribed, as "informant" is relative and is friendly –the good type. In the trio-negotiator segment you will discover that informants give the team footing edge, they give the team what the team needs. Anywhere they can get it, they will go.

But as the negotiation dialogue progresses, there is what I call re-touch, a situation whereby the components rub minds together –information. This one is giving the other the latest, and the important, and refreshing themselves. You should always have it as a team function.

Why should this re-visitation be? These are information, useful hints, useable analyses the one has, which the other mayn't have. It is always like current, recent development. Team-hood is all about links, connecting to the other; and refreshing the other, so we utilize the game when we play most like the team. It keeps your team on and refreshed.

The informant has done his work, but the deal now in the market at the hub of the vestibule to its paradise of dominant could refer again for a properly mordant analyses -re-touch from probably the same informant. The point is not losing control, so we improvise anything we can even when what we can can't directly lead, ability is something you can borrow to lift any weight to keep the lead.

Time factor is a serious advantage in negotiation. We say, pending on the circumstance when we have wasted the time we ought to have utilized in profiting our target; never nullify the rule "first things first."

While business explorer was inside doing the business, setting up pillars that can hold the company, the ticking hand deflected the impeders, they lost the finally, the last breath could not be pumped out -life has gone, a new king was emerging. You know, you can delay a deal perhaps it comes to your terms, and you can hasten a deal when you are at a favourable end.

> The most effective way to maximized time is when you have the product knowledge, the market game, understands the chance of your product and objective; and still know the market's priority and taste.

See what the business did: there preparation modus Vivendi could not be infested, they got prepared from home to market, market to home, and relocated from home to market -they became market resident. No chance was given out for any breath of thought from any sort of intention.

You use advantage to gain better advantages. However slim or crumby an advantage is; the fact is that advantage is advantage. Just see it as the chance to make better use of doing what needs to be done, and not sell off or postpone a work for a rest. If you have followed the narration so far you may have noticed that the businesses were busy working. It was a restless working. No play, no jack and no dull boy. I, as an opponent can sell your advantage to anyone or in any way to void you of plot, but not you.

PERFECT PLANS PICK NEED

At this point I have to recap some vital notes. When you want to position and create an advantage, there are things you must pick to erect up as advantage. They are: time, the business knowledge, competition [quality, price, and service], and the competitor. Build these, as your edge of advantage and not as your goal; and you will have ever-access.

This whole equivocation and realities of fact was how the business house, the very fort of your empire of business was built. The simple reason why the business chooses that location, which is in the likelihood of our needs and interest, is because that is what they needed to establish their dream; and they dealt on it as a target. <u>Excuses are no more facts that justify our failing, it does not justify failure. There must be reason for success.</u>

Don't wrangle yet, please. Let's continue our story. It will soon end.

It is so obvious that the business has invaded, and hopeful to receive and build castle in the space after the last planet, with their concern -target. As a negotiator you must learn to remain positive, even though situational difficult deadlocking may burst up. Facts are not always the truth. Some of the negotiating masters have told us some of the way out from deadlocking deal.

> I will be very unrealistic, if I tell you it goes without discreet aplomb. No, but you are   an intelligent staff, a superb-thinking because that is what it takes to beat challenges.

The entire fear, all the reasons or causes of the whole fear in business, which we jump into through deadlock are one thing -lost, we don't want to fail. When it triggers too long, looks impossible invading it, we don't want to go the available way because it is not going to give us what we have anticipated. But, if we know sufficient skills to burst deadlocks we will not fear what an effigy that may be placed, or molded on our way.

Visit information warehouse; think out, amalgamating every piece of knowledge. Solution is always around if we can still believe. Before you agree to settle for deadlock, take from your opponent what will make him, her or them come after you, take confidence from them, leave them with the fact that you alone has what they need – useful disguises. Not that there are no similar satisfiers, but what they need is with you. This is the impression you give them. But make it real, if not completely, to an extent.

Business was a stand point. The opponent rather than doing the real work of an opponent, they were busy following business trend. Business pioneer(s) gets every pace before they can get anything. Business was ahead of plans –general market, customers. Product improvement, projection to the opponents, resources were spent, risks were taken, guts were imbibed, plans were encouraged, appraised and actions were not ignored –no part diminished, or lacked, business initiative and team-hood was strongly motivated.

How ironically interesting are the two intelligent negotiators. They mustn't have been sent if they weren't seen fit for the spy-work. Must have had the same kind of training, read the same books, and rules, and exposed to the same skills and mentors; but see how the goofing guy goofed. Don't consider trivia if you haven't got your goal.

Prepare your concessive material before hand and work in order of the vision. Doing what you aren't set to do is an indirect way of saying you never had a perfect, trustable, and convincible preparation.

YOU GOOF, YOU GOOF YOUR TARGET

As we continue, we have to forgive the spy [intelligent negotiator] who went in to negotiate the unknown with who, and what he does not know. There should not be such thing as negotiating ignorant in negotiation. Since the eruption was mysterious, the opponent assumed it was creatural rather than mystifying the business. Therefore they allowed it, an opponent that has the potentials of turning you to a past glory, to develop to its fullest.

The last series of business rule tells you what to do when you are in a market or environment that allows anybody with any business, whether competitive or not. Because the zone has become so compromising, conditional, and heartless it has nobodies interest but [market is] insincerely with a naive opinion.

Relinquishing your stand in the market because that is either the trend or what seems to be unionist agreement, hasn't always been a standard counsel. It is good enough if we remain nodding in the market, while refining and re-birthing the dream. That is to say you finally concluded you were wrong <u>so you can re-dream</u>. They call it ad-venture, which is modification of brand; in this, there is need for difference.

> This is amongst the many things that differentiate success from co-incidence. Success is a built skill but co-incidence is an impromptu of luck.

I think, if it is creatural i.e. natural about the eruption, then it should be also natural that you live in the market you need. Have dream-gut. You need it. I have never seen a dream live without either breaking boundary or seeing a terrorist.

At this observing time, one asked what my observation was: "honestly, it is not preferable to negotiate the unknown with an unknown. The dabbling is un-salvaging wreckage; because such experience is costlier. But if it is a must, be carefully the best negotiator." Be like them with no difference; but don't sell your heart.

> Cracking the walls of the experts to possess a portion of the market, taking over trend from the leading trend perhaps, winning peoples opinion from their favourite, is what the case has been, if you know, allowing you a portion is shortening their arms of profit.

Being more realistic: how many times have you made a comparative proposal to the market, and was void of success in-spite the best you did? Every proposal is buyable; people only flinch at it because it might be made better.

However, somehow so mysterious, somebody you never believed could be offered the deal; or could have being the one you dreaded most, the one you hoped he/she is never given the deal, or ordained to lead the market, got the offer. And many of this instances, we prognoses what is called "nepotism". Effective negotiation is permuting a decision like nibbling. It commands the way.

Remember you are target oriented. And if you really are, don't give yourself and your target lapses. And also, don't believe [relax] on the excuses. One thing I know is that it takes skills to beat defense. However they got the deal, the underlying is that they were pushed by the target to negotiate best. No dealer would give you the room you want except he sees clearly how it will achieve his/her interest [target], and this is your effect.

Now, the business has come and dominated the market. You will never be what your dream is if you follow the business' steps [imitate]. Imitations in the market are what some stand negotiators do to frustrate and exhaust a product before bringing out their plans. But however, you have to have some uniqueness that cannot be understood, at least till after your goal.

And you know, when you continue to win with the same strategies; it means you are at a retarding point. And because you are not challenged yet, you can't notice it. Majority of conquerors conquer with weapons that are never familiar, something they can't soon and easily find the cure. Hit them, and leave them in the recovering Coma –a better word for this is confiscate.

Fighting competitor with a familiar tool is an indirect way of self-woe. The computer manufacturer, electronic producer, and mobile communication net-workers around the globe are examples to this. Coca-Cola and

Pepsi are like niggling 5 and 6. All are because of the clicks in the conception(s). The luck they have is that no competitor has come into their midst –at least, I can tell this from what I learned from the business clan, which you can understand [what] from the "business rule [competitive negotiator]".

Brand dominance is something you make in the brand way. Honestly you have to read the referenced above *"the competitive negotiator"* and experience what is called arts in negotiation, the crisps that never break and yet can lift the weight of the world; the movement of the giant. Brand does not model brand. You must make your brand with dominating forces, things that cannot be found outside it. Of course, there are still strange things happening – strangeness is simply doing what is not expected, not thought about.

NOTHING IS IMPOSSIBLE

The wall is so high. The width is so thick. And the foundation is so very solid and deep. The fame echoes afar. This colony is grand in the market. Huff would say you are not fit to stand the market especially, looking at the port folioing entourage of your opponent(s). You are not capitally intensive, knowledge –nobody has ever being an isle-land, no speaking connections or influence equal to that of the opponent, come to be now, when anybody can access anything anytime before one can know it.

Moments like this in our chicken-nature, we give our targets the uncalled excuses. Yes, it might be good to give our targets excuses, which are the conclude-able issues in our hearts where we try to get self-acceptable convictions for some foul decisions/actions; dwelling in shoots of fault(s), may be your opponent should by dent be in de-ovation.

It takes gut to negotiate with this market where you have different and pulling contra-opinions! Denting one's image to ride over his seat in the market isn't a sociable finesse for a healthy environment. You mustn't denigrate. It has its back effect, gambit rather. You must develop qualities of good success, which to add to all we've known and mentioned, is acceptability.

> Survey statistics shows that every brand has its taste as well as desire, and audience. So if we can channel a starter we might find a standing point. The presumed competitors are still so frightened.

As I watched, I was noticing it all. Please, wait a moment: don't forget the owners of the territory. Business remains so and only invasive. The territory initially belonged to the loosing team. Whatever could have being the reason while business are taking over the territory, I can't recur it now.

However, some of the things I know is important in leading us onto establishing our targets includes: business are like figments which when they take over, they take over and very difficult to pursue out. Even most time, you may end in damaging what you wouldn't have wished to, in efforts to put business off the market.

And secondly, the loosing territories could have lost bids in the market because, either as the sayings goes "if we don't see needs we may not understand the importance of what is available." Or maybe, intimidation, and suspension activities has only being shrinking their nerves. One thing these do is that both have the intuition to mute skill.

Could it be the effect of re-occurrences? You know, there are ways a thing recur itself in-spite the plugs of efficacies, you will still slightly feel like thinking otherwise. *You are either a business or you don't allow business into the market.* They can confuse you and make you lose focus

The problem that is beating you off-feet is simply the crisp you flinched and called common. I believe in being thorough, making sure to stone is left unturned until you achieve the target; and continue it till you seal the deal. When we say "thorough" I mean everything that makes a thing, even the systems. Be sure of security.

What I called flinch here is not on what is the target. It is the combination you assumed you don't want, neither the goal wants –what you should not have flinched at. Security and back up is one other thing.

What you do in your life is supposed investment; and you must negotiate everything about it thoroughly. Lapses are what brings failure, or loses; so this is what you negotiate against sometimes. Then, you build back up in case of any eventuality.

And, you don't belong if you won't rehearse. Be constant in the business. What carries approval is measured by value verse nitty-gritty. So be en-gut with the pride of liberty, and rule your world. Your brand having the major is basically you: internal and external bases.

Negotiation is all about beating through if necessary, and chatting with respondents to achieve your target. Avoid giving your goal excuses, reasons why it can be postponed to a reasonable time, or can't be realized. There are ways to keep business going.

OPPOSITE REACTION

Let's negotiate through: [the competitive negotiator]'s markets developed a law called "opposite reaction" where three elements are involved. Namely: you, opponents, and the market. Market, needs, demand, and audience are in the same class. The need is the most essential thing, the common reason; while you and your opponents are coming to do what I called liaise with the need.

The law is simple: when there are two forces coming to take the market, which cannot agree. Each, better be on the opposite. I.e. if you are at this end (A), your opponent, to ensure there is market equilibrium and appreciation, it is better you come from the other side (B). In as much as we have always tried to do it the other way round, but this is the real thing that goes on. It is about coming to terms, a language, an understanding. And this is the negotiation.

> Your ability to push the need to a state of deciding which to follow in the market is an echoing fact that if only you can do extra to what you have done you can dominate the market.

Therefore, I see the law of opposite reaction as a tool of pushing the need [market] to the room of decision, strategizing you or either, to rule through efficiency of brand [goal] management.

I have told you about negotiating almost with the need, gaining the market; but let me ask this question. Have you ever negotiated with your opponent over his stand or weight in the market, even though we do things related to this, un-identically? This is the acme of gut, which situation may call sometimes that we carry out the negotiation. For you to take your stand, you must do it [somehow].

The phenomenon about dealing is a thing, which must be imbedded in satisfaction: either satisfying the market or chase off the else possibilities for the market to be satisfied; indirectly blindfolding the market, so we could remain the only brand in the market.

This is not perfect utility. This state of negotiation is heart pricking, anything may happen and all you have spent years to build could just be a waste, wreck. You will have all to lose: dream, name, sociality, fun, appraisals, profit, increase, standard, and satisfaction, all could be ruined when things turn like this –when any notch pushes up into the market.

You will learn to manage both the bullet and your glass [delicacy] when you have built [names]. That is what the world is stylishly. Bullet and its sender have nothing to lose, they only want you out. And so you protect your glass from breakage, and still try to be safe. And you know how painful it is to know that bullets have neither respect nor memory if you were nice.

Referring within our business story: you know it is one thing that you spy me in other to displace and replace me. And it is another issue that you gut-fully approach me to step down for you. This is common among politicians and most companies that buy-up some company in other to share freelance to establish their brand or interest. What I have come to understand is that money can buy and so cheap anything that does not know its value as well as things we give as concessions.

This security against the bullet and the shooter is more sophisticated than all these insurance policies they recite to us. It is your adept negotiation that secures this.

However, it is a very perfect [direct and efficient] way to beating competition, and controlling the market – monopoly, a market with one leader. Need ought to be in control of the market, controlling the players; but because need is starving and bleating for satisfaction, which you might likely be the only one in the market platform to provide, you manage the need.

Need always fails to rightly boost its image, it runs after anything, appealing offer(s). It is the worst to treasure, worst to neglect, and the most to make one feel good or bad.

NO BAD OFFENCE IN BUSINESS

Having known the major essence of competition, knocking off the distractions is not a bad offence relatively. And since the absent of competition makes what is available in the market viable, we may not do the business without offences. Suffices to imply that the only reason why your product or service, what you offer is being strangled and rejected on the table is because there is another one satisfying the need more than you are, taking your place; and perhaps has done what you did not do. Or maybe you have not gone to your market.

Provide your deal on the table of convenience customer-compatibility, and acceptability, and close the competition. There is a deceit here. Sometime we don't really get to our market. We think we have; but we are yet to reach, and communicate with the market we made our product for.

This becomes much a case to do, if your path finding is good enough. Remember the good/bad guy's gambit, a tactful concept of behaviour just to achieve an objective when there are fouls around you. I can't forget a story about the CEOs who complained about a new brand taking over their market.

Yes, there is brand liberty in the market. And choices are optional. But the only law I have learnt in shooting is simple enough: "in as much as that is your target, shoot when you have to shoot and don't talk". The problem most of those chief executive officers had is the cloaks of their systems. Their systems are so rigid to the extent it began to discomfort the market, the offers are no more appealing; the market had to go out to seek for alternative(s).

This is true. Market can help itself get alternative to its pleasure when the businessperson makes it wrong to rely on that business. Provide your game plan on the seats of convenience so they can sit long enough, satisfying you, making you a company of pleasure. Because, it is awful to be without your pleasure, life doesn't go without it.

Competitive dialoguing table is aim and shoot, nobody will wait for your slobs. No courtesy in shooting. Because there is liberty and equity of product, what I expected those CEOs to do is to give the new invading manufacturers a direction, direct them to where/how you want them be, and make your brand very much, and more a cloak on the market. Even the bible talked how Elisha led the soldiers that came to arrest him to their enemies. It is not an offence. Create an urgent and intense room for your product/service order.

You do this when it becomes impossible or hard to compete. Be the good guy/bad guy. Pull your competitors to the dialoguing table. Don't relent and don't relinquish, and don't miss a shoot. Remember your aim is to make room for your goods/service, having scads of contact with the need.

By this you will see the efficient power of "better reality". Take them [opponents] out from the market if that is your choice with the power of better business reality. And, you can even be the biting business who applies the "law of activities".

DON'T ALLOW A BUSINESS IN TO YOUR MARKET

Pray no business negotiator finds your treasured market; because, if they find it, you might lose that treasure. Most of the trade unions: these are what they do –controlling and determining the market [need] and the brands. What they can only control is the product and services, and maybe positioning through their laws and enforcement. Not satisfaction.

Though we negotiate with them, but you can make it possible to be the market master. It is better to get little and get the market on for you in-spite how rich your product is than to have a competitor around [whether strong or weak]

> Satisfaction is always traditional in every market. It is intrinsic, not a bodacious conglomeration. Therefore, try to control availability and status-quo of product management, and directions of demand in your line. You will do this better, if you realize how the market is a prostitute.

The mistake has been made. [Business(s)] have already taken the market, even though you are still niggling and fluctuating. And, it is quite hard to take the business out of the market; though they are like viruses. You can either choose to be, or not allowed into your territory. The damages will cost everything cost-able both time, and energy to recover. Imagine the intriguing coma the territories were, even from when they noticed the eruption began?

Your spy has gone and come back with the report. The entire body goes to plan. It is now very much obvious that the coming negotiation is with the opponent, and not the need, which will be a very interesting and peace dominating, if only you can conquer the opponent. This is because, when you beat off an opposition in your market, you will have peace resolution and reign. Opponents make it a wrestling cage, a kind of hugger-mugger.

Aardvark in accordance with plan, were of opine to disengage or occupy the business –abstract activities; even though they were yet to know the real owners of the dominating protrusion. Sometimes poor action can be fruitful if we accompany it with little wisdom.

They planned to pollute, and disorganize the opponent's settings, by infusing some "spooky gaseous elements". To their conclusion, this would enable them truly know the dominance, and maybe, know how to take them, and other plots were engendered.

One other thing you must do is this: as a dominating crew always expect everything from anywhere, even the worst. And when you do this, you get prepared for how to stand in-case the worst happens.

It was a blast like a bomb; and yet, so spooky. The blast pulled their attention, and the smell inconvenienced them so that the business came out in battalions. These are situations we find ourselves in, when our positions either the office or in the market is attacked.

But if you are always expecting everything to possibly happen, you won't be tensed up when anything happens; because, you have prepared a good and safe way for yourself. The unfortunate thing was that when soldier ant(s) burst out, tortoise and co were still not gone. They were caught as the plotters. Business were not only sensitive to their environment but, to their game. Sensitivity made them come out on time, to catch the opponent, a trace-able line, a clue to an in-coming competitor

The territories hardly believed business could be such magnanimous, terrific. Remember this Mr. Negotiator, as an augmenting rule: do not disdain your opponent, in-spite how beggarly and weak they may look, even when they impress with inabilities. What they do in critical times is to give an impression. Like I told you, the only order that must lead you, is your goal.

Learn your opponent for the sake of advantage and machinations, but not to give you direction. I know that what people see, hear, read, and smell has a way of distinction, which tomorrow might become part of settling contributor. This impression is whichever way, and in however forms.

Tortoise and his friend [I don't know the name)] never noticed when the business leaped on them sarcastically. And with awesome tone "It was not easy," they said after they had managed to escape the bites; especially, tortoise, in-spite the shell.

But you know what? However uneasy it was, the factual reality, and latest on ground is that business are now suspects, and also, few business were eaten.

The first spy's cumulative system is now beginning to read again, many and blistering meaning in contrast with what he saw under the tree inside the tunnel and little ant that came out to squash. This is quite an incredible dealer-hood.

Since they have known that soldier ants are the treasure holders, trend leaders, and wishes, designers; according to their inference business can be beaten. It may only take them time, which they don't have. But, looking at the scene, I believe time is not their only problem. The problem I have so far is that, even if they should have all the time in the clock, it will not still give the winning over the dominant. Their problem is [very, very] poor negotiation. They don't know it even though they are doing it.

Most times we think negotiation can always be done. When we do it without knowing it, it will end that we give away our fortune in attempt to possessing what we never intended giving out. Before one can succeed in a thing, such must learn it, know it, and do it. This is just what I believe is the source of their [business opponent] goofing.

How should this have been an unfortunate advantage? As a negotiator, especially in this regard; you should have positioned time, advantageously, and prepared for both the advantages and offers. Although, time is a key factor, but when you are prepared and know it [the game] you can always have the time. This is because everybody living always can make out the time from the one they have.

You could create an immediate deadlock and as well not be bothered if encroached with deadlock if you have the time. You simply relax until the opponent gets tired and call it back; or maybe as seller, the buyer may want to go round, abandon the deal as though he doesn't want it. So you just allow them to stroll and still return to buy your product.

This, you do unshaken when you have the best product and wowing service that they can pay whatever it costs to own. When you don't have time, you lose negotiation quickly. It is better you build a standard and meet a long-term target, than pursue a short-term target without a standard.

Time factor will always be on the advantage axis when you work in order of plan. The mistake the other animals made was to allow the business settle, even when their home-based work has no decency that survival can appraise. They came when they were ready; whereas the invaders are stronger than they were. And that is it; don't give chance if you must take it all and good.

Reptilians were awarded the contract to eat up the business. Indeed, business are soldiers that spread attacks, and more aggressive than viruses. The bites alone on the contractors though they wrecked very much business, are till tomorrow as I talk with you indelible scars on those oppositions. It has become an everlasting stigma, a remark.

You know what? You can't win an adept negotiator. Imagine the attempts opponents have launched on the business. First was to scatter and confuse the market, contra-dealing with market against the business' standard; now they have just finished awarding another contract – they have probably found out that business can be eaten, swallow and they are no more. This are just to take a market, yet, the end is almost near.

> Solutions and success is not by the strategy, not the formula, the systems, not the rules or principles. These are like frames, plans, and steps to achieving a target. All depends on a major fundamental. The most things that count, and make all these: wonderful, superb, result-full is how we carry these things out. The attitude is the key to all that. And we can, as a short cut to the attitude, get things done if we choose to understand first, why are all these things involved.

When the neighbouring animals could not conquer the business so they can possess the treasure, they proposed to a group of foreigners, who inverted the bid: "it must be fifty by fifty before we can help you". Is it an agreement? It is no more one holder, but partnership: "we help you with <u>what you need</u> to establish your goal and you will give us equity". All they both want is same –market share.

Even the foreign companies can see their flops.

Foreign companies [all country's companies are foreign to other countries] have always done this, maybe because of their developmental advantages: many of American/china companies are taking their share in their kind of market; currency appreciation replicate. Business-wise modus-operandi in the kiosk of its modus-operandi is not left out. Trans-continental deal upholds this lot. They use their prepared and knowledge to seize advantages.

What are they doing? Reserving a portion for themselves in your market they help secure for you; and yet you pay them. Study and get imbued with business' rules. It will help you. *Understand me here; I applaud anyone who can help you get what you need under conditions from anyone, even foreigners. It is the advantages they have over you they are simply costing. The business would have done same either. It is about costing [your] spills*

Sometimes, people don't easily appreciate costless value you put on them. You made it so, and because it is so always, why would one then, bud to spend on what can be gotten free.

DID YOU DO YOUR BEST BEFORE INVITING MARGIN CUTTERS?

Do you have house to deal on? You need products to sell, but you neither have the material capital, nor much of the intellectual capital: no money, no goods; inefficient skill, and minimal experiences so you proposed for capitalization? This is smart enough, especially when you need to seize opportunity.

Margin cutters can be the supporters –foreign bodies you invite to help (do) business on your target. They could be investors/partners, they could be any other parties with where-withal to getting your target –they empower you and your team and your target with what is needful. But because of the conditions of deal, most cases we lose what we stand to gain. Terms are often at the mercy of these merchants of liquidity and bravo.

Is anything wrong with the foreigner's proposition? No. Is anything wrong with the territories accepting the proposition? No. But I think somebody is not negotiating to the best of the ability, which I think is the effect of psyche. Learn to be boundless: vision should be boundless and timely. Not bound! *[Ref: entrepreneurs from tunnel]*

However, external body is always external body –banks do this: investors will always look for where to invest because it makes more profit for them. But they only do it if you are worth the investment [content of your proposition]. Your negotiating proposal becomes worth if you make the presumed investor see what he/she would want to see. You know the phenomenon? People act when they are convinced or subjected from their mind.

They draw out policy for you, however it is; you are the grease in them. As every sound machine needs greasing to function fine, likewise every investor needs viable market to invest. While you look for investor to invest in your proposal likewise they are looking for where to invest. So don't let the standard short your mouth and don't wait or make them see your foul.

Establish a perfect dialogue and let it wangle little. The foreigners set up the policy? Fine! Negotiate over the fifty, fifty policy. Tomorrow you could get the whole market. Not bad, but there is nothing bad if you don't lose at all today. Just build your gearing mind on winning the negotiation.

Despite the un-palatable nature of the proposed bid, the animals accepted without firstly refining the terms, thus hiding their fouls or playing without it –Curiousity. Imperfect dealers are curious minds. Provided they have a state, recognition in the market of all need. Note. This is not bad, and it's never the better.

How can I make you understand that the story just began? How will the business [the ruling brand], and the entomologist [the foreigners] play the game? It just got tough, tougher, and toughest. The fifty over fifty bids is on the possible outcome of the foreigner's effort over the business. Business are adept, stunt, and impossible. And the opponents have groomed enough to the extent that I can't asserting what will be next, the game may not end well. This is like foreseeing what we say "spoilt game"

Because of their entomological experiences and knowledge, they knew business' likeliness. So negotiating with business is not a too much an issue. Though they don't understand the terms of the business rules but they can to over average level [predict] business.

This is the same thing we say: you can't negotiate in ignorance. It is not professional. If you make any fortune it is luck, which will not be fixed, stable. You must be proven. There is need to know all the knowable! In this stage of negotiation you either chase them away or they chase you away.

The foreigners firstly cracked down the business wall, wrecked to bottom. This act scattered the business. It was like pre-awareness for the change in market helm and trend. Maybe the business' might as well be gone from the market they have equally suffered too much attack. But, no one cares, not even the bullets do. Interests have nothing like feelings of sympathy, or compromise.

Some of these we come to live in, threatening our market and progression. However these Businesspersons are still seen as the best. The brand and need for it have being so attached to them to the extent that only dynamic uniqueness can cause the change. Customers appreciate this attachment; they can't easily stand opposite, except they are made to do so.

Business were seen as most genuine product that gives real satisfaction, the market have not seen any problem with business. They are very much okay; not even conscious of the willingness to taste other problem because of this effect. And because of the peoples confident over business influence, not too long after desolation they rebuilt the wall.

Entomologist knew that business have that capacity, and the unflinching skill to do that very well. And if they continue like that they may never get an audient, let alone having a satiable fifty, fifty stake. On the other hand, the market could see both foreigners and the animals as chatterers, team without vestige [reliable trust] and foundation -fake. The problem is this: the opponent and their entomologist were like strangers, their systems and general operation sounds so [foreign] to the market.

See; if you want to get the market, don't give the market the room or impression to read in you what will not buy you in the market, perhaps, a kind of insinuating foreign, because foreign no matter what have a home. It will cost you wealth of potentials to wash on, if at all it will.

The employed negotiators had a brief dialogue and concluded on what/how to handle the business, but still with caution. Skill development is vital.

They decided to chemical the wall in such a way that it can penetrate and collapse the foundation possibly. You must learn to uproot from the foundation or else it will grow back and still inconvenience you. When you take over a place, ensure you secure it. Therefore don't rely on second chance; do it right the first time. This is the meaning of their plots.

This has nothing to do with confronting them. You don't need to persuade the market without valued tangibility either because; somehow in some cases persuasion is not totally reality. Better act of persuasion is satisfaction, validity, relationship, and always present and eternal. All that is necessary is going to the heart of the need, the deciding point, a liaising medium -what I need and what you need. Strategize yourself properly and be ready.

Every need has neither familiarity as transactional archer, nepotism nor its flare. All needs look for is just one thing: *will you always be there to give me everything I would need or demand.* So business has the market because they do this to the market; thus, satisfying the need and secure the market. If you must get it and retain it, this is what you do.

What they [business] have being doing the whole while is security. Otherwise, there were product and transactions that could have been satiable, if it had the chance to be in the market.

This therefore means that it is not only an issue of satisfaction to remain in the market. You go extra miles to secure your lots because, **as a law of market competition, it is an inferable tendency that every product that finds its legs in the market will definitely have a dealer.**

Your product is good and service is excellently a wow! But if you don't govern your community well enough, someone, maybe an opponent will be willing to keep them for you in another apartment. So security is like giving your destiny the favour it needs from you. Who could have believed that the wallowing fins of negotiation extend to even this "security"?

So when the "entomologist" finally had the access to the power basement, their identity was seen and tasted, they were recognized. Now, if you don't have any security over your host you are bound to lose them.

One thing someone must not think so sure is that your clients will not definitely taste the new satisfier; but security, which is laid on the hutch of brand [product and service]; will keep them within your vice.

The chemical paralyzed the wall so badly that it penetrated the foundation, and voided that part of it that was affected. This is common: <u>weaknesses and limitations are shared secrets to disguised friendship</u>. And business were beaten by the entomologist because their secrets were spied out. This led to the clan's rule **"cost your spills"**.

Where and how was the excess spill? Were some business eaten before now? Does the entomologist know something about the business? Maybe there, could be the sniffing port through which they got to the root, and learned a treat from a client. Anything is possible.

The limitations you see that led to "the collapse of the wall down to the foundation" are, because somebody, a seriously prospective opponent knew the secrets to your brand success. This act was like a boundary between the business and other satisfier in the market. Don't always make your competitive boundary conspicuous. And, remember the coalition law between the need and the two satisfiers called the law of "opposite reaction" in the market.

The business still have two third [3/4] of the markets though; while others [foreigners and the animals] shared the one third [1/4] of what they got by fifty, fifty according to the agreement.

Concession is not the best tool in adept session to play with, though we must when the need arises. You may not believe it but it makes the game not be thorough, while you keep on liaising with an opponent, unknowingly rubbing off some read-able moles on the opponent. And negotiators don't lose at all: it is a game of, you win and I win. Or you could win, and I can as well win the deal.

Book "1"

BUSINESS FORCES

Sure we all know most of the taught rules in negotiation: somehow, "Don't Ok the first offer", even when it seems good enough. "Flinch at proposal", you never can tell what may happen. Don't slash because cutting down price is not the best key to making your deal, and all those rules. But there are better and deal making force that can work it. Every business has its force -what makes it prevailing, strategic, and outstandingly unique. This are what makes a business be. It is not about the ideal but the ameliorative package policy makes a business, it designs an ideal.

These are elementary issues that we boomerang with. But what is the nitty-gritty of the rules that stands as intrinsic as insignificant pale, I mean rules of analyses. These are the business forces – The Omen of substantial reaction. These are what we shall deal with –although every business has its rule but there are rules are generally –they are applicable in all finesse

These Business rules are kind of proven tactical steps to achieve what we want to achieve just as we want it. You can't define it; you can only call it rules. The hoax of negotiation reprimand mordantly that this rules be passed to every negotiator. And it is open to everybody so that all can have access to it, and negotiate their deals very professionally and good enough.

These rules are not only applicable but are result-full in negotiation. We have known this game of negotiation as a diplomatic[29] skill of/to satisfaction. There is no other prime factor the business forces invigorate except making every of its candidate "Adept negotiator".

An amazing syndrome I see in the life span of venture is that most often, rules have always existed without attitude or explicating approaches, leaving in lines of

---

[29] Systematic way, most often indefinite

consideration fallibilities in ventures. When the business gave me the rules to cross-relate it to the globe of onus, there were quite some emphases about their attitude; because it takes attitude to bring out fertility in a model.

So the only rule to applying business rule like business we would do is, **"if you can't imbibe their attitude, don't apply their rule"**. Attitude reprimands, it commands you into responsiveness; you can't if you don't have the attitude, and you can if you do. Therefore every rule has its attitude that makes it work the way it is expected to work, being the applying factor.

Before we go to the business place where the business lives, and pragmatically swim across their ethos-at-work, here are the business place[30] reviewed rules. It was necessary that this reviewing work be after the fallen of the world most famous business empire; and set-forth this rules.

Remember this fundamental tract-analogical[31] scenario: In negotiation there are no "want to be", and there are no "feelings"; only rules exists for the negotiator's team. And the rules are as simple as this: **"Get the deal done, and don't be tamed."** Sure you know what it means; you'd better not gone, than be tamed.

---

[30] Company, business board and management
[31] Sequence of conglomeration, systems of occurrence

The market is balanced: you may learn the "want to" and the "feelings" Scenarios to manipulate with it to getting the best, but not to build your decision from it. Negotiations I know are politicking, and in politicking you plan your goal, accumulate to reserve better chances if there are no way while you pave the way, but when there is a way, shoot your best shot. This scenario is because of the market communication[32] and the opponent's communication.

Action produces responses is in the line of communication, you stand as a meeting point between your market and your opponent; they communicate to you in their diverse ways and languages and you are expected to respond in like manner. As life communicates to life, so also presence is to presence, actions to actions, and need to need. All communicate to one another. This is the way to know the attitude of the business

In this nutshell it is as inferred, not necessarily swimming with the fishes in the river that we look out to be, but being the biggest and best fish in the river is the pride. I just hope as we review the rules together, you will understand the place of competition and cooperation. And, the reason for this is to enable you position your target in midst of negotiations. How?[33]

---

[32] The interactions between all that exist [in the market] and how the move to do it
[33] When you put your target in midst of negotiations first, it means your target is the general interest –they bought the plan to work for you while they know they do for themselves, you can stand if like after you have blown the whistle, while they play the game , anyone who wins hands the trophy to you. Your duty is only set the target, set the rules for a team, show no

Team is a union, target is competitive, but team can have
its target –don't give chances when you have an un-met
target. You are not being smart, the simple homework to
do is understand the propinquities between nice and
target, business and pleasure, team and competition; and
separately, why give the chance? If this is not done, in a
way one will goof. Other preliminaries before we read the
business creeds are the Business attitudes.

BUSINESS ATTITUDE

We will see the important of this if we realize that it takes
required force to get a work done; therefore attitude
[approach]   plus   rules   [formula]   equals   solution
[expected]. All the business has ever achieved is based on
these, their plans, pattern and targeting –will give you the
insight.

It is called for, imbibing the nature of business because it
will help all neophytes[34] play the perfect business. Can you
tell why in-spite the works, efforts to program and
terminate business; if they don't rehabilitate, they still
build a new empire in the same environment. Even,
before we can deal with them they would have gained
what they want first. Giving the right attitude to a course

---

interest if you like, but allow them play like they know themselves as real opponents. Don't
interrupt the game or any motive. Winning can be possible even when you don't play.
[34] People who learn, apprentice, new trainees, we never stop learning

can make the course as real as it is in the dream-world, and the wrong attitude can make it never to be.

Knowing these attitudes can interpret their mood, their spirit, and their skill: necessities for motivational. You must learn the art of choosing your attitude "intentionally" for the sake of the target. Sometimes, the environment would not demand the right attitude –attitude that favours the target; but this is why you are the player, to decide and choose target-success-attitude in-spite the factor behind the environment that is not favourable

Attitudes are the spirit of motivation for the goal. To some people this is so ironic to be true, but that is the business for you –we propel motivation

It is not what they want you see, what they want you know and not how/when they want you do a thing. It is all about shoots that project and calculate your goal. Remember we don't disregard their notch. But be sure what you see them do is what you want them do soon enough.

The environment is not favourable because the systems within the environment demand it to be so. One of the secrets I have learnt is that right attitude has its way of dinning with system crooned environment, so to the best we are concerned with attitude: there is no difference between situational cold water, hot water and ice water. You can live through if you plan the right attitude. The secret effect of this is that it gives strength to your gut – mind.

Business "adept" negotiators have no other attitude chiefly than goal-centered gambit-tactics, chosen attitude that motivates the goal. And they allow themselves inured with that attitude. This inurnment is because nature is nature, once it is, it happens naturally[35]. Don't do it like a student learning principles.

However, attitude is never generally universal. Choose-able attitude should be attitude that is effectively applicable to the environment, attitude that can buy my opinion; or else you'll be seen as malefactor, who will not be allowed. You will come to the business rule "natural" for more explanation. While some are general, although some are uniquely applicable. But because of environmental differences, study every environment and give it the rightly goal-crooned attitude.

Attitude is the opium, the energy, the boost to getting things. However our business rules are, when we understand the manner with which business execute their jobs, it magnifies the efficiency of the rules. Anyway rules express somehow the attitude but how is the nature of their gesture. It is not just shooting; it is being the best and perfect shooter.

---

[35] According to your target, anybody can use words they wish like luck

- Target-centered gambit-tactics
- Cleverly humbly and gentle
- Attractive
- Courageous and consistent
- Tenacious
- Positivity.

.......to list few

RULE NO. 1
THE LAW OF NECESSITY:

This is simple:

"DO WHAT IS NECESSARY NO MATTER WHAT."

Defining what is necessary is another strategizing way that enables you to excellently utilize every instrument and potential chances; knowing what to retain, and what to dispose, where to position a thing and when to use an offer, or give an offer –all these are hooks of necessity. Although we talk target, but there are environment where our target may not be first to declare bluntly. There can be occasion of set-up

Clarifying the necessity of everything, and giving to all the required effect implies you know what you are doing and understand every system of your tool; especially towards getting your aim. You must not be rolodex, that is playing silly sainthood, and you must not be perfidious, being unethical; but just gray: honest and Business. Any assignment you are not comfortable doing and must do it, delegate it to your environment

Learn to reserve and plan on necessity; don't misplace it. Necessity keeps you in purpose, reserves promotions for you; necessity is always in the place of question: why are you here? Why are you doing what you are doing? Why the whys? Why are we asked or employed to negotiate a deal, why? The opponent made his offer, but you refused it, why? What is your target? Where are the chips? And when is the nick? Why the action and why the sequel?

I often tell negotiator: it is not seeing that you do a thing, but what is the value [honour] it adds, and the guiding principle. In other not to be tamed, you must play according to rule. Life-wise and organization-wise everything count per value; what you add to them, they add back to you. Defining value puts you on optimal utility.

Necessity becomes unnecessary when there is no significant value or improvement in the statues-quo, especially where there is a standard already. Therefore we must firstly point out answer to the question, which defines and build up the walls of necessity, before we can understand and ameliorate the necessities.

This is the episcopalism[36] of the business rule of necessity: adding value to a course according to the pattern or policy. The worth of a thing is much in the value it adds, the difference it makes. Business rule on necessity predefines this value, because it define things in its order

This business do: they are not compelled by what you do, they are compelled by the plan of the house; because every envisioned plan has value it adds to the goal. Therefore do what is necessary no matter what.

Negotiators are not people who bluntly venture on everything or people who dabble, and hoax on; we know what we need, and how to get it rightly. Of what necessity is the spirit of win, win in a negotiation be to me if at the end I am not getting my goal? When I have no goal anything becomes ok, but when I have, it is the only ok.

RULE NO. 2

DON'T VIOLATE THE POLICY
BE SMART WITH THE POLICY

There is different between trans-generational and generational. What cuts across all generation and ages is boundless -modus operandi; besides, success is not stumbling. It is a living system.

---

[36] Lordship, reverend, adorable relationship

Everything definable must have a guiding (defined) factor to be termed success. Professionalism does not count luck; it counts successive sequence. One's ability to adopt is a cling-able anchor of trust. Organizations easily hold on proficiency –they make out the policy, you uphold the policy, even yielding results. This rule makes you an adept team member.

Policy is the leading of every objective, if there should be frame of organization, it is the policy; the only thing that base model, it is the systems that is put in place to guide the functions of the organization. This gives us view to the inquisitive phenol; by this I mean those questions of discomfort in the processes. And if it is something consciously made in lieu to organizational aim, it mustn't by somehow be among what should be tampered.

It is rather better being a conventional negotiator than a circumventive dealmaker[37]. Your first step to principle and progression is policy: disciplinarians' attitude and honesty. You don't break target for reasons, especially for lowly scored necessity.

You flout your[38] honour directly or indirectly when you capitalize on powers and chances, veto and egos; probably you have the opportunity or maybe the CEO, or head of a department or with a deciding mandate. And so you would be seen as what you are in the organization, at the

---

[37] Dealmaker who avoid the responsibility of seeing that the target is achieved
[38] The integrity of your policy

call of your position, you answer to your place. Most occasions, this is what makes loses: the authority, the power of the deal is easily known.

This is called flaccidity with rule, a situation whereby an amateur leads a rule; but [un-diagnostically and in rolodex][39], the order of order, the word of the leader is the constitutionally agreed policy, not the sashaying views.

The claw here is that you can't decide over a thing except you are in position to make the decision, and these are people who occasionally forfeit mandate whether because situation calls for it or they are that carefree favour giving type. Once in hook they are scared of loosing so they yield; and others stamp on to be recognized -they must be there to yes their yes or no their no, even when chances for better prospect are still much prating for the negotiator.

Opportunity is one of the craftiest finesse I have ever known, it in a kind is beguiling, it makes you make decisions; but however, acting in impulse or not on adlib cases isn't necessary. There is a laid down principle, a pattern to every existent, and in every existence, doing it the "Watson way (Tedlow, 2003)" according to the rule is one rule never to fail.

---

[39] Without any refining, mincing and sifting words with the lip

This has neither conceptual propinquity nor dialogue with radical marketing. Radical marketing is the boiling zeal of goal, projecting in the lane of principles plan whose essence is the goal.

Rules are meant to fulfill and not to impede the goal, so it is allowed to crack a rule not accurately proposed to achieve a target. This is like taking the gut to break through market with high fence, and thick slab foundation; or maybe releasing an order on credit even when it is against the rule. It is important to be a radical marketer; nothing can always hold you from fulfilling any target well understood; but there are no policies without goals.

As a decision maker, your yes or no matters. You must not allow SUGGESTIONS –it could be from people or favour or influence getting into the system. When this is done, the company has opened the beginning point to loosing genuine and appreciate-able value, especially if you are care-free. No, not so; I don't mean you to be a Jack of all business. There is what we do with suggestion(S) –they are criticized and finally developed to fit in.

The clamour and luring influence will come, people will do it without you calling them, and all they want to get in is your association. At this time you become the target of most people's action, nepotism, and un-hearted acts feigned to win your trust.

Remember that there is hardly an organizational rule without the conferential inference. Always analyze your decision in ratio to the goal.

Truly, some rules are opposition, hindrances to the goal itself, they stand as rule, obeying them are like going against the plan. What is missing here is the understanding of the rule's attitude, rules here are not what those kinds of separate statement we make as a result of daily experiences we encounter in the running of the company and make rules to guide it another day. Real rules come with the goal. Is like saying goals hailed from rules, such protects and speaks goal

Despising or taking for granted your policy whether because time is in your favour, or you have broken your down-line before your client, or simply because you must make a deal, maybe others are blasting deal, you haven't made any for long; the only chance you have has a blemish and flinching conditions that flops defiantly your policy. What-ever the case is, rules exalt the goal. Foul-goal is foul. In the field, the referee will blow whistle against you.

Breaking your policy will only place a limiting clause, expose your loopholes and confidence, which will give both your clients and co-competitors chances to relegate your value. Flouts like this show inefficiency; like you ought to know –once the referee blows whistle against the goal you have achieved, you know what it means, soonest, you will be on bench, which is another way to understand the whistle lingual-franca.

The beginning analyses here is why the only chance would come with blemish and flinching conditions that flops defiantly your company's standard, or that ridicules your company? Secondly see if your policy is justifiable? Third priority: is it that money is made, or product is out with very little profit [turnover]. Can the chance satisfy your target, the integrity of your company? Then ask yourself –what is the existing value between standard and target?

The conclusion of all the answer will give you what is necessary, as necessity makes you see what to do. People are stunt and impertinent-able; therefore to deal with people successfully you have to be skillfully stunt. Remember the vital skill in "success stories" of Robert kiyosaki –ability of progression.

You don't always have to break the pillar of your house to increase status quo unless there is a change in planned target. Necessity demands for necessary actions. One insignificantly natural attitude (phenomenon) of deals is that there must always be a standard, a level, a class; so whenever you place yourself, people will rank.

Out-running your policy, either by doing without it or altering your policy to suit the moment exposes two weaknesses: Curiosity and non-professionalism, which does not give you the position in the market, you are subject to situation. Envision goal doesn't plan situational, they plan control; if it is a short-term goal, they give it short rules, and if it is long term, they give it long-term rules.

Since curiosity and non-professionalism are exposable weaknesses when we break our rule, is it then too bad to be curious for good things? It is bare to live without curiousity, but you lose ground (advantage), when you can't cover your curiosity. This is in negotiation-wise, especially when you meet a deadly negotiator like the business; you will be screwed. Exhibit the attitude of control

Curiousity can never be dignified. It is just posing, flaking. Let the person see a defining integrity, a controller margining devices that are specialized in intimidating gut, the curious mind will be so humiliated when it is all been said and done.

To conquer curiousity, you must have time advantage and knowledge. You can never be a good negotiator when you are too curious, therefore learn to organize the use of time in the advantage portfolio. Oh! You don't know a defined integrity can intimidate gut? The foundation of gut is the mind, and what is in the mind? Knowledge from different sources is in the mind.

What do you think makes the bankers and port folioing entities dress corporately dignified? It is just a common image they want to portray, unknowingly intending their dignity to communicate their confident and favouritism to your nerves and tenses; and when you see them the only voice entering your ear is the "image". Moreover because of the caliber of this so-called posture, sometime a more experienced dealer leads them back to negotiate the modification of their goal [policy].

Policy should be unbreakable: your target should be your first policy. When adept dealers see that your policy is not going to help them use you, they revert; leading back to review our goal, imbuing your files with the market is up with, and also modify you policy. Until after this, they will not sign-up deal with you; and these people get so easily confused with the "treat your customers right" or they tell you "customers are always right"; and these people never asked who then should treat sellers right, or are dealers then to be treated wrongly. The best way to treat a customer well is satisfaction.

We don't argue with customers no matter what. When we know they are wrong, we upgrade their psycho-state to enhance their effect, their reasoning[40]. We treat them good enough to remain in business, not shutdown after the last client. Always try to get your deal done without crack your rule. A rule that can't work can be noticed from a distance. You do not need to come to the verge of

---

[40] Book ref: "sell yourself, and earn the whole world". Same author

ending or succeed the deal before noticing the rule is wrong; maybe an understanding is yet to be derived.

People defeat you when you defeat yourself. Policy is like your word that sinks in people's heart: this is what kept Business in the market –system. They were definable, not confused branding, trend followers; even brand imitators. They have their brand anyone can know from any distance, and there system is so rigid, you can't easily crack the code to disorganize it.

Note that the market[41] was not truly willing to let the business off the market, because they have been able to place definition between their needs and the business; business became a value-able, un-give-out-able asset in the market because of this –policy. [Target has its way of positioning you].

It should be obvious now that market leadership[ii] is not imitation, imitation is just someone trying to play smart, and such has no resilient substance. People go to people because there is something offer-able, so they rather go to the real owner, than keeping with fake, you become manageably valued when the real is not in the market.

What are the key issues in the standard (policy) function: Not confusing your brand with so many ideals –be definite. This is not brand utilization[iii] –chasing market, because you can't catch it. It is better you prepare, and attract it like with a trap, let it fall to you.

RULE # 3

WHAT YOU ARE NOT SET FOR, DON'T BE PULLED INTO IT
-LEARN TO BE IN CONTROL

Adlib is a magnitude for sole-quest. We won't conglomerate that by the concept of the third rule, we don't handle spontaneous indulgence[iv]; part of being in control, is "not been taken unaware, but sometime taking prompts unexpectedly." Being able to tell illusion, impression and elusion in transaction marginality is management[v].

Ideal can never leave pace for allegories. Brand and vision definition tells what is and what is not when your brand mixes into the market. This is essential because of the rapport system in negotiations -taking things in a full concept of negotiation. Brand is the product of vision.

Moreover, as we are treating something you don't just go into like that. You have to know your product (brand) and market; market and competitors; and product (brand) and competitors   (imitators).   These   three   groups communicate, and are what we pioneer[vi].

Identifying this format of knowledge; knowing the differences and the interns sets your preparation. This is why you have to be an adept negotiator, smart type, which relates your ability to get all those information, always ready to succeed any beat beyond the usual. If you have plans, then you don't have anything that can take you unaware; because your plan is your major concern, which also determine the relevance you put on others notch around you. What are the plans[vii] you've set up for the steps to your target?

One of the things we teach about negotiation is to be in power, and you know being in power is all about legible transposition;   politicking   consciously   is   sometime necessary, not the thug. You are not in power when you are with such an adlib pull into a deal.

Power[viii] has a way of absolving an impulse (pressure), commanding and change the status quo and uses, like a slave. When in power you must learn protection and investment, because power is asset, an opportunity [advantage], your value, and your respect. When your power is protected, you don't talk of defense or offense. No, you only attend at suit, and determine as necessary.

This clue shows the [pro-verging][42] intensity of power. It is all about saying that: if you don't have it in mind you can't do anything better about it. You would have done something better as you wished, but you can't because it's not in your mind. Your power mind-set affects the way you act, reason, present yourself; not follies but the weight it pulls. What this implies is to know your worth, your caliber, and using it in negotiation. <u>What is the bargaining[ix] power</u>; an attribute that qualifies or certify you for what you are asking for. Know and strategies the necessaries

It is a good luck to grab opportunity, and sweeter when you are paid for not working[x], but also what has no standard depreciation; show the world your standard, your worth, and they will pay the regard[xi]. Always make sure you negotiate what you have in mind with a reasonable amount of dignity. When you can negotiate better and your dignity is speaking audaciously, there will be no much speech or act before the deal ends in your favour –remember, it is about carrying the mind of your opponent.

Following the business beat[xii] can take your dignity away. The flail ability of power to use everything, either by prank or not, insinuation or not, direct or blunt command, is insignia. This is the intrigue about it –it works on people, even after they have swore that they

---

[42] Substantial, extra, the force of dominance, control, confident

would not obsolete[43], they can't believe seeing themselves bow to power of such kind, whatever is reading in their mind is not an issue, they have just allowed you have it, which is the work of your power.

Power advantages are not what we make a show with, flex or get too frenzy in. it is necessary for the necessities; to keep things under control[xiii], as planned.

Who then borrows power? What makes you a person of the people is not callousness, and not how clumsy, phlegmatic and simply you can be used. It is the active dignity[xiv], the personality you attach to the concern. I know most politicians to be good in this clumsy ovation, yet no dignity is attached to the people. They know 'the' politick and so they play the game. Show-case the acceptable difference[xv] –Sensible things knows their differences.

The two simple truths are that you are either in power by mistake or understand today's lessons tomorrow. Don't mistake this exposure with access. Keep and execute the plan as targeted.

However, there are systematic issues in life that requires systematic or conventional approaches, and there are some you must improvise or rather use unconventional discretion[xvi]. But any of these you may chose to, carry your

---

43 Leave the market, be dominated by a power

dignity, and let it [dignity] carry out your negotiation in midst of your plan.

Power is nothing but in the permutation psychology of all acceptances. Watson making people (his workers) do things Watson way is the simple psycho-syndrome[44]. I mean: This is how adept negotiators (Business) win –they control you; they subject you to a limited or rather, minimized decision, actions that are proportionally prompted by the influence of their effort or force.

And as soon as you remain in their boundary they won't mind leaving you in that spell. You are yet to be the negotiator if you can't control your competitor.

Somehow sometime they get you stranded, and most time they keep you in suspense presenting them like opportunity – an offer. They give you an offer and you see it, map out strategy and starts to work on it, un-realizing you are simply working in the plan (the offer), under them.

Somebody should know how it is normally done! You meet soldier ants[xvii], get bored; in bid to kill them you follow their rail. Very good technique: follow till they are found guilty (enter). One major issue in this is synergy waste –misdirected utility.

---

44 effect

Birds know when to return to the nest, know when to refer back to the target plan[xviii] so you can always remain in order as planned; people make mistake often when they are psyched. Since we know power is capable of collecting power, we must learn how to bestow power upon ourselves. We give ourselves the power first, before it can collect others.

There are one thousand and one opportunities to things; either you educate yourself to standard with power, or you create more results. These are all forces of influence that attract respect[xix]. With full conviction I will buy into the ideal that you know a successful target by the level of its plan or preparation

Negotiation is just an honest game, and this as simple as honesty can, is that they do what they say; while you who don't understand would call them names that real gamester would bother sitting under. Real negotiators don't bother much about this, because everybody has it, some good, and some bad; even good people bear bad name. It depends on point of understanding

Remember the rule "Better realities", but the frank point between this is that adept negotiators don't give keywords; that is word that can either link or engender impediments to goal, expose or narrow their plans and decisions, or perfect still hooking words[xx]. But what they say in gambit they do in gambit.

You are expected to know why people hold people by their words. Because of this they don't bring their words close to their target, rather, negotiators pack dust[45] into the air so you can walk through it, even trying to figure out what is going on, maybe before you'll be through, they are gone, guiding their goal, making way to the top.

Remember what I told you: pick everything in the environment, but don't set goals by it. Superb negotiators are known for this. Disguisers; and you are simply OK with peanut. Don't they make their target known? They work it out themselves, sometime using the environment. In their craft is their target.

This is another characteristic law of power[xxi] – you can get anything you want to get, it doesn't insinuate trickery, but your quality of intelligent, guts, awareness, and skill: say what you mean to so, know you can do it, and do it, because the rule of reality is more active than glue. And you know sometime reality measures integrity. People keep you in mind and even follow you when they know you to be real[46].

Therefore pre-occupying your opponents or challenging mind of decision with activities doesn't mean untrue or dishonesty. You are simply margining out the game of

---

[45] Dust >activities, zigzag and most looking irrelevant

[46] The key to their satisfaction

concession. Give them activities well like a welcome-to-show.

> Concession[47] is a very strong will that allows you
> to have anything you want. It is the popular rule
> of give and take. Learn to in-signify your target in
> the mind of your opponents and challenges
> through concession, and signify your target in the
> mind of the need trust and capability.

The business story you will find under "guts in negotiation has underlining with this: The entomologists[xxii] that came to help negotiate between the business, opponent, and needs in the market discovered that this was one of business major device that has kept them as market choice.

The same thing they had to do after they might have succeeded to chemical the business' home [gambit the business position in the market]. Or else, insignia disallows, and leads confrontations in groping search for means to defile the legacy, or you will be locked up for confederating.

RULE # 4

---

47   See crack standard win negotiators, page 167

THE RULE OF ACTIVITIES:

YOU EITHER KEEP THEM BUSY, OR THEY KEEP YOU BUSY.

There is nobody without a plan and no time without what to do, but sometime people act on impulsion, interceptions. It is simply knowing and organizing people's buyable opinion to their notice. The rule of activities is a machination of one-third (1/3) of business rules.

As adept negotiator, know how to create activities for your challenges, or opponents in occasions of interest ratio. Keep them busy in the order you want them to be, relevant or irrelevant, orderly or ordered zigzag, just project issue for them to crack, hold their minds/intellect under rule. Condition their materials in favour of your will; make it large and deep and tall, attractive and suitable. So that before they could swim out into the oceans of realities, you are gone.

The simple reason why an opponent or a case could be like thorns in the flesh of the team is because the opponent has the free chance. He is void of activity, so he, she has and they have the allowance, the room to machinate and exploit.

This rule is helpful especially when you are not prepared, even when you are faced with deadlocking. Note: when your opponent knows your aim, the next is to check the pros and the cons it might be to his, her and their interest, before deciding what to do with it; but know that if you are a sort of hindrance to them, they will want to pick you with a stencil off the way.

Activity doesn't play the winning for you; it only makes the way free and opens for you. Some of the time we spent yo-yoing[48] within concession can be saved if we understand the incredibility of the rule of activity. And you finally either put forth your hand to click on the button you have long waited for, or circumstantially, pick the pen to approve it [seal], or in another area you just simply institute what you want after your activity has led them to the Dead Sea

When you know what bingos need and how to throw the bones to them, having your way is not going to be your problem in negotiation according to the referred book "competitive negotiator." You know, "...just throw the bones to the dogs".

You know, dogs do not always know the where about of a bone though it always wants it, can smell and possibly trace it. Since we know how much bingo loves bones, will it not be a good plan organizing bones for the dogs –as many as possible?

So it would see you are worth appreciation if you pick a bone from the ground and bingo the dog [impression] –it

---

[48] Playing business like toy game that goes up and down –real word "yo-yo"

finds it quicker than the search and satisfies the longing. If you need it to be out of the way for too long, then waste the bone for the dog to where none of you would have to disturb yourselves going through; after all who cares about the waste bone if not the bingo. And if just to have access, you may not have to throw the bone too far, at least you may want to collect the bone again.

The distance between you and your target in this instance is first the bingo zone. Know that. You know how desperate a starved bingo would be. Make your conceding offer to the bingo portray its expectation.

To the best of this: the bingo is satisfied and happy with and for the bone if in the course[49] of the deal it has gotten such an interesting bone first. Because the dog would believe with all amount of coax that they can still get you another before the time ticks off, "maybe another day" so the mind will say. Therefore would take it and count you a looser, posing and wagging its tail in pride over you.

Make the bone attractive and very much spiced; something that can't be refused because some bingos are trained with defiant detector[50] vaccine to read mood, and refuse accepting bones from strangers and mimickers.

---

[49] Also, process
[50] They know all oops and want, their target is always on their mind, attempts to change their focus can put you in trouble, always alert against concession

The only thing that takes you through this stage in your negotiation is confident: it hides loopholes, and schemes. When it barks do not fright, just keep the move and cordial. When you do not show stranger signal or smell it will see you as family member who maybe traveled and just returned, the next you see is friendliness; and you know how to handle such a friend very well.

I can't just imagine it that while you are almost to append your signature, to cross the crispy tinny line after you have done excellent negotiation for what you want to buy, only to you hear a very loud negatively horrific sound: halt! Or whoa [Bark]!! What is wrong? You are about to lose the game, trend is turning, a threat has come.

> Well, whatever that might be wrong; the fact is that confident has its way of approving a notion and silencing a stop.

Hope you realize this is found in the fins[51] of concession? If you must achieve your goal beware of concession.

I enjoy concession, but for the fact that I can't figure out interest propinquity between you and me is enough ware when accepting your grant. Comportment is an efficacious fleet of any entity –I do not line by it. It has a way of tapping into decisive factors, emotions, and resistant of the receiver, leaving your target in the hand of suspended

---

[51] The packaged pattern, and gliding sequence

fate, you may name it abandoned project, when it is accurately positioned.

So therefore reviewing the rule of activity, we can say: if you can lead or project an issue or opinion into the heart or people, there will be a suspenseful dominant, which has the potential tendency of keeping that person in wrongly planned goal, out from self use to your use.

The power of activity[xxiii] is so efficient that it un-doubt-ably burns energy whether time energy, material energy or intellectual energy; activity uses all energy. This is the negotiators power skill, make up files of different and similar activities to use; the truth is that somebody cannot hold you until he, she, or they know(s) how to, and what can hold you, and where to hold.

Like I said, activity only makes the way free for you. It is like having penalty shoot without any qualified goal-keeper on the post. It is an unusual skill, making your opponent lose focus from tacking you. And when you have entered the gear[52] of motive, fire the engine[53] with the discretional ability, as the vehicle[54] moves on to where it is ordered as necessary.

Did you realize that activity made the opponent not to know when/how the business built the foundation? If not

---

[52] What can make you move at different motions, ranges, and   circumstances
[53] The corporate and complete body that enables function/chances
[54] Team business

that chemical[55]; neither the animal opponent [your competitor that wants same thing you want], nor the human opponent [entomologist -third party negotiator] could have known until the end. Real rule(s) has no respect. Even the ones who make rules can be ruled by another person who understands it.

The rule of activity can be used by everybody and on everybody: staff on boss, boss on staff, interest on interest; it is a disguised concession, which you can use when somebody is not given you what you want, or refusing your plain offer.

Before we continue with the remain rules of the business negotiator, know that business rules is only to make a firm negotiator, and wining negotiator, build up unprecedented standard. It is better people know your policy and would want to give you the maximum respect, than dabbling around with you.

Establish your standard, define your goals, and get equipped before the deal begins. One of be things these rules does is that it keeps your opponent out from using their intelligent rightly; they can't psyche or make efficient plot.

You may understand this better if you realize that when people have nothing doing, they become workshop for

---

idle works –instruments of freedom, responsible to nobody, obliged to no rule, and ready for anything appealing. But when you make them responsible by doing a work for you, they will be useful, at least to you

COST YOUR SPILLS AND BALANCE THE GAME

People are intimidated and cramped with lures and incapability: lures from the opponent and incapability speaking to them of their shortcomings. But adept negotiators know that every notching in deal is enthusiastic, because, even the professors of psychology can still be psyche.

Always rate your product, whatever you are offering; and remain in the threshold. People will want to intimidate you so you can sir them, but negotiator's gut is powered (stirred) by challenges [obscenity] if they can know what they need to know. So reserve your dignity.

A brand ought to be an authority by all standards. When you have nothing, act like you know what you really want, and when you have it, let it be like you know you have it; because the price you give for your product as selling price is what buyers will act on, maybe pay for it.

At negotiation line, know when/what/how to talk/listen. Listeners sometime win more than talkers. To win a negotiation table is to program and count your spills; you do not need to be an orator, giving out everything through every means while the opponent sits and count for you. It is neither accent nor what goes out, but a simple and applicable tactical skill of getting what you want. There is what we call "Power talk"

Power talks are your verbal expressible efforts that conclude and guide your opponent's decision; as soon as they hear it, action follows; it becomes the opinion: first, because that is what they expect to hear from you; and secondly, if that is not what they expect to hear, it strikes their need antenna -power talk [often like persuasive words].

However, if you have chosen to use multitude of words as disguise in your dealing, it is your skill, this doesn't still a mule like power talk does. I use words some time, but I'm very much careful; because talkers are not always the winners. Poor sales marketers are good in this; they end up sales presentation with multitude of talk, yet do not know techniques of commanding sales. Sale is not by talk, it is by techniques built by knowledge.

I told some of them I recruited for a company I worked with a time ago that "if you recite those marketers' lyrics like every other marketers they[56] will treat you like others, but when you act uniquely, you will be treated specially." And that is the issue with selling -the same scheme.

---

[56] Customers, clients

Products are products but differ; all have their unique selling formula that makes it easier. All you just do is discover the formula and style for your product. Selling may have the same basic but different uniqueness and formula.

Marketers have their jargons[57], and some buyers know it. Some know the way it sounds, and others know it by terms. *And note: buyers don't want these jargons, they want something, and you should know it to sell them. Telling me you are a marketer from so-so and so company, this product is the best I have ever seen that preserves your machine" are prolonging the issue, wasting the little time I gave you. Specifically selling on identification, using the right terms[58] is superb.*

And like I hinted, buyers have their community, as well as sellers. When you get into buyers community speak buyers tongue, put on buyers attitude, and treat it in yourself without any exemption of supposition. Keep your jargons to yourself; you may use it in your marketers' community, not in buyers. They don't understand that language; it scares them. You must speak buyers' language to get a buyer; it is very swift –it connects in splits of seconds to get whole of the time you might require from a friend –buyer.

---

[57] Words or forms of communication common or familiar within a set of people, association or group

[58] Customer's language [I want a car with central headlight]: - [this car has stylishly designed central headlight, just look at the way it lights out], key words that satisfies and makes them know this can give what they really wants.

I was shocked one, they when I beheld a marketer feeling so unwanted, inferior, hated and rejected. Why? A prospective client, one that is worth ten thousandth turned him down.

That was not my surprise. What I asked myself was "so even marketers feel like clients?" I thought only buyers have that sense of recognition; that regard, that lordly nature. All the while I thought customers [buyers] alone should be treated right. Most sales-marketers after some level of turn-down, they do not like encountering the same client again. Marketers, deal-makers I think we should ignore them and their insults –they are lads, babes.

And, like I was on before, since everything go by interest, they look out to see what would be of interest; and they hook to it. This is why we warn negotiators to beware of words[59], because it is the spirit of hope, it can easily stick to the mind [consciousness]. You are either held by it or you hold on it. Most dealers over talk, and don't know when they make some deal, or spill excess. They are [cut and nail][60] negotiator, who doesn't know how to close a deal.

One of the first things you should have to learn is how to close deals; very important. The difference between marketing and sales making is so telling to the extent that

---

[59] The promises, assurance, commitment, things you say to get the customer's ok
[60] Unskilled, untrained

something, sometimes; we spoil our opened sale through trying to market the product. Most of the approaches we use are like knockout to the deal, they spoil the deal and its chances. It makes you more useful to your dependents[61]. Utterances and some of these things we say are only to make way so we can seal the deal; don't impede your deal.

Don't expose your incapability by not knowing when/how to seal a deal. You realize how bad it feels like if after all the skillful gambits you believe to have displayed and yet you can't close the deal[xxiv]. In some occasions, you must need to call it up to close the deal. Some dependents are good at that –waiting for the call.

Deal is the core reality, not [activities]. Enthusiastic is like a prompter that stirs up deal striking blade, even sometimes smartness intimidates your opponent in ways that adlib, the deal just seal-up to your favour.

> What is the point; cost your spills when you concede. The friendship you make on negotiation boundary is because of the deal, the target: help them to keep the relationship by giving them a penguin shout, while you consent all to help you keep the deal. However you make this, *don't let initiative take the place of purpose.*

---

[61] Who you are dealing with whether buyer or opponent

And also, don't destroy the friendship you built in course of the deal, even after the deal for many reasons [human value, futurism of other deal]. It's worth keeping.

Cost your spill[xxv] is all about personal or team skills and attitude management and advantage management in our deals. Like the story teller told us; concession is not a best tool to play with, but sometimes, when necessary, we have to give bingo[62] some rubbish called bones.

RULE #6

LOOKE NATURAL (because natural things are real)

Conviction is the only thing that commands approval; whether it is buying of trust, or yielding, satisfaction, or whatever that has to do with contraction between two entities. This was a personal experience.

People try to be sometimes realistic, analytical, and convincing before giving into a course; being as natural as earth is the only thing that leaves resources at your use. Nature is, when it's time to be hot, you are; and when to be cold, you are cold –unsuspected. People are very alert like a very powerful computer to detect any slight change or foul. But nature have always dumbfounded them –it is the worst to follow, and most indefatigable

---

[62] Second series –Business rule: competitive negotiator

Therefore, because of this [watchful dog][63], you have to be normal [naturally in mandate], natural when you ply on the abnormal region [cross boundary or living the territory of the opposite]; don't be subject to event(s) even if you must behave like Rome when in ... We all know actions have its way of communication. The truth is that there is no way a cultured watchful dog can allow you go through when you are a suspect. When it totes and bark, be wise.

This is the rule in the business clan that presents them incomprehensive: you neither understands nor controls it, just revolutionary. And because people known nature is more real than fiction, ever revolving, they easily conclude about you, and clang on with impressions, which would lure them into spending their capitals on the wrong thing entirely.

When you are this; people won't easily notice your secrets or any changes, because they will see it all as nature and handle it, like you are reading this book will handle nature[64]. And what do we do with nature? Apply it, especially now, when it is becoming so easy to believe that "you can't cheat nature". You position them with no minder to manipulate or stop nature. People, in these days do the best they can, but leave nature to itself because they believe "you can't change nature".

---

[63] Alert to changes of any kind, anything suspect
[64] Normal, what do not need a tamper, sometimes hobby, pleasures of time and events, what will be will be.

Review the business story, and notice the nature of the business-spy. This is one of the rules that can keep you void of attacks and interruptions, because humans tends to nurture nature, especially [phlegmatic figments][65]; even most jeopardize their stances trying to fortify this "nature[66]", without really understanding what is in the heart of the "nature".

We business negotiator, the major reason why nothing seems strange to us is because we know life is simply, mind exposure; we make what we need it to be. There is no effigy anywhere called nature that has not changed at least, once. All have their other side, which might be conducive for us. I mean why do we eat woods and walls if we don't know there can be another side? And this fact has always given what actually we want to get.

To get this rightly done, you must learn the entire learn-able attitude, because attitude is the bedrock of nature. Where do we exhibit our attitude? It is in the environment, where can we likely exude and see these attitudes? And like we have it in the Business attitude: "attitude that is useable is attitude that is applicable effectively to and in the environment."I give-in because you gave me what I needed, so that nothing really goes for anything.

---

[65] What can't hurt or do any harm –innocent and weak
[66] Supposed challenge, opponent

There might be no end list of attitude but like I observed in business clan and have approved right: right attitude is attitude that is goal centered gambit-tactics [manner]'; they don't use it like it is a practice, but it is in them as natural as breath. Culture every attitude.

RULE # 7

THE INTELLIGIENT WEAKNESS

Remember, one of the major essences of this business rules is having your way through with the deal as planned. Opinions might be, but may also not be true. You may not be weak truly, but people's opinion might say you are weak. This concept is far from the general norm that "first impression matters". This has no propinquities with feebleness. We simply show abilities, willingness that look up to partnership, reliance.

Don't always show the opponent the strength except the gambits. Impress the deal itself with your strength.

Intelligent weakness is tested gambit. Closing any deal is also a string of cloak, but a cloak you carry and wear on your opponent or buyer or seller; it depends on the side you are. And when he, she or they gives you a power either in consent, or descent; appreciation or commitment manage it well.

Because of some reluctant[67] dealer you must initiate a technical pull that will always draw them in to give the last bid whether in money or commodity or whatever forms you want it. All gambits are to boost, vaunt the value of trade. Therefore give devaluation or deadlock to any reluctant dealer after you have clad on contentment.

Intelligent weaknesses always have its pass, because it is a drone. If not the existence of folly, we could not have easily distinguished wisdom. Give a persistent rattler this scheme, and you will find out why he, she or they rattled. It is normal phenomenon that every defense you see comes because there was an offence, in other words offense calls for defense. There can't weak-side without strong-side; but when you foresee tough game, soften it with your persuading invigorating weakness. It is sometimes better than hit to hit, thug to thug

Nobody will bother to exhibit intelligent, strength, or skill on weakness, feebleness, or a drone or novice. They will always want ways to boost or motivate such but first would come to eat from it, so they could do something for them. This is because, the name is weakness.

Therefore, we pose a form of weakness to opponent [not as opponent to them, because, you don't make opponent know you are an opponent except you have to], using it to

---

[67] They give impression that means no interest to what is on, or interest dies off quickly especially in the middle of the deal when they are expected to be more interested.

lure them to sympathy, helping, and not unleashing out their full strength on you, in-case it can kill you out.

Visit the car dealer and notice something. They have a way of dealing with you, especially when you go on negotiation with them. To get your whole conviction and probably collect as much money as they could know you would have saved, they allow you sometimes to have a tip test of what you are about to buy, make you understand how business had been so unfortunate, using their your desire to sell you. And the next thing, you are already test-driving the car.

And you know how whisky this can be? They tell you to just feel the car or plead if you can be allowed. They can, so they do. In your mind all sorts of gratifications are accorded to your ego, and their customer caring quo; but you do not easily realize that you are giving them advantages they could not convey to you with words or any other means except you test-drive and accord it to them. It is woe. Your grunt sold you.

Maybe you return with "wow this is marvelous" or sympathetic feeling. They lure you not with their strength but your pride, loose-control [you became soft for them to penetrate]; indirectly your strength became strength they can use to pull you. They don't need to show how strong they are. You alone can take decision they would have made; it therefore lies in your strength.

Intelligent weakness is not showing them your strength, your approval, your consent, you're Ok. Negotiators who want more satisfaction don't have Ok. What they have is push-more [josh's gambits]. Push on with everything possible to lay hands on until the time stops ticking. While the one who give mark-up continue the margin? When you offer to split the difference[xxvi] according to a friend, you most cases, indirectly and unknowingly, divide your right, your advantages.

It is called intelligent weakness because it has a diplomatic way of sucking energy[68] from your opponents, reducing their force, postponing the launch of their strategic plans, seeing it as not the type, caliber of dealer and deal, and time they should use their major winning key. They must have seen you as "the weak type"; but you know you are strong, even stronger than they are, just allow them to wallow in their mild ovation.

The simple end point is this: they are convinced you could have one or two things to add to them, may not outsmart them, because they see you are weak, which you know it is not true, they can let you go, but they can't walk away from you. They are bind with a cloak of what they can get from you, desired from the first impression you gave them –you have stuffs they need, they can use you, you are willing to work for them, if they will like to make a difference with you.

---

[68] Time, gambits, possessed resources that ought to have help win the deal

This is what you see in most clients who are without fundamental background of the field and environment [the deal-type concerned], and so to get your consent they augment to their portfolio a buyable impression, which you would see and appreciate to live the reality. This is not bad to encourage, they are simply negotiating their goal, a dream to live, but if the spade can go deeper, it can dig out something that may be like gold.

You remember what transpired between the business and the market; you know the markets somehow study about business. It was never in the mind of the market that business should give the foreigner 1% of market share; the market was perfectly Ok with the business. The market never knew how much the business were using them to build a sky-scraping castle[69], even while the market has fallen prey.

And, from another point of view, the market would not have enjoyed benefit in mixed-branding, mixed branding is a better a way to keep a market apace -being refreshed with multiple choice, innovations, and enjoy cost-friendly. But in-spite this goodness, we sellers do not gratifyingly welcome it, because we know no one would be truly without plot, be happy losing interest. And sometimes, may not be original interest.

Every negotiator like I said before, have the capacity and know how to create his, her or their market, either in an

---

[69] benefit

existing market or not. Confrontation is very good but does not avert the intend-able risk. Leading the bull by the horn, even with bully is never safe. The principle of synergy is all about using others or extra effort [energy - energy that is required] to get a thing done.

Intelligent weakness is an arm scope of synergy. But remember the intelligent weakness. If we can enthusiastic with antitragi[70]; incapability is the superintendent to our intelligent weakness. Yes, when you can't then go learn it, but special learning has no special preparation. If you know what to learn, learn it when you find who can teach you, or where to learn it.

Most time we negotiate, it happens between tested intelligent (teams we have had deals with) and some of this time a strange huge hand comes to shake our hand for a deal; the common phenomenon of playing on peoples intelligent is making them believe they are stronger than you, therefore using their resource materials; this will somehow psychologically re-tune and strategies their flaming claws, reducing it to pinch.

You can only quench fire with things like water. While you project your target, lead your challenge to leave strategy. And this you can do by affecting their readiness. Look when you hold a business, how would you feel quantifying it with what you know business is really capable of doing? That is the intelligent weakness.

---

[70] In with good or have some goodies

Businesses are intelligently weak –you would not want to harm it but the bite tells you the opposite of this.

RULE # 8

EMOTIONABILITY

This is all about the infiltrating strength of emotion, the extent to which our ability to use emotion is indefinite. Emotion as generally believed is weapon mostly used by women, and they coin it in the shell of compliments. It is still a powerful tool amongst business people today.

Business are purely and cleverly emotionalized negotiators, not either timid or compromisers. Something I have always understood about negotiation is having your way with your target; forget the concern they show to your interest, you are only been gamed. As there is interest in every value so there is interest in every concern. But when this interest is shown to us, we don't either reject it. We use it with interest.

Remember there are times you must be swift, and there are times you must numb. There are times you crack on, which may give you way or bring deadlocks; and there are ways to avoid deadlocks in deal, sometime it is good you create deadlock to build favour.

Emotion is a humanistic comb, and force on which they tend to act majority of the time. This serves as a perfecting virtue that accompanies your negotiation physique. A well emotion negotiator always have listener; and listeners are good followers

People – either side should understand this emotional infiltration, which is why sometimes, consciously and unconsciously there should be some magnum[71] of craft; as a matter of fact, learn how to tap into and on emotions.

Controlling emotion is like controlling mood/tendency; and catching the mood is like understanding the intelligent plan/decision. In whatever you do, be emotionally intelligent; don't break emotional rules[xxvii], which includes that, *if you know you don't want to be willing to succumb don't show relevance. Emotion buys willingness.*

And secondly, *every emotion is subject to alteration;* therefore if you must mimic, prance, bash, and phlegmatic to arrest emotional attention, you better do it. There is no shy in romance, only pretence. So use it like you are proud to use it in getting what you want. After all, are not matured enough to use it?

---

[71]Pulling force, magnetic, powers

There is no way you can get things as proposed if you can't handle the emotions. Talk when you need to talk, listen when necessary, refuse when you feel a conviction is devouring your advantages/profit, and demand without penitence. "Ask for more than you can get" so that at worst case scenario you'll get what you really want.

To be a better negotiator you must learn how to use and conquer emotions. You use it to win a deal, and you can as well conquer it to maintain an interest, because you are not the only one reading this book.

On a second wheel of thought, emotion could mean that one is either weak and can't resist persuasion, so have to be Mr. or Mrs. Nice; or one could be that angering type, easily provoked so can't maintain tempo; these all have pros and cons. Either of these can make you lose a deal or tangible profit, or the side of the thought -contrary standpoint is. Perfection begins with the ability to applying the right tool right to work.

Rather than this, be politely firm. Be driven by goals. There is no being nice in business, but good, better, best; or bad, worse, worst. Be the excellent in whatever you choose to be.

Why would the leaders I spoke with in the business' clan include this in the "business rule"? I believe they spoke from one their books [knowledge] of the best teacher. And, the title of this book and the page or chapter we can get this fully, they promise to give it before the end of the training series.

It is totally a different thing to say one is emotionally poor or intellectually poor. Emotional poverty follows a rim with fallibility. Men of great intelligent fail because they are emotionally poor and often challenged. Beat those lapses. Ability varies: intellectual, material, emotional, financial, name it; to do well, master the prime keys. These are the bases of bases, which includes highly, transposable intellectual wealth. You can use Emotion to cripple intellect when you deal with anyone. No statues humanly categorized have flown to mud emotion.

Emotion as we talk is in all rounds with persuasion, anything that disrupts ethics as in the business concerned is emotional trap. OPM[72] is a term I first learnt through Robert. Kiyosaki, a tangible proposal is enough to pull someone to tender. How? The pile sinks into the psycho-emotion-ability of all you think is, blazing the analyzing intellect, which might either approve or disapprove the proposal.

This tangibility must accompany an approving proposal: business nitty-gritty, features, and remunerations, total plan. Other People Money is a key phrase in fundraisers package; and they need it for what they do, satisfying the requirement is never going be the issue.

---

[72] Book by Robert kiyosaki

RULE # 9

PRAXIS OF BRANDING
ONE BRAND, DIFFERENT WAYS

Nothing thrives most than what is in its praxis uninterrupted. Interruption is what we should plan for, not avoid. Business environment calls for it.

> Business' clan is a model to all brands. One and one set of employees but different sculpture. Not similar.

Your ability to continue as intended in-spite this is mastery. And, how can we continue when we are interrupted? Interruption has types, and continuity also, does. Interruption could be of any type, but we must ensure our continuity is not on any opening, but on the real plan; because the plan can lead to the target.

Competition will ever exist as well as market fluctuation. When there are no challenges the market can never be fair or balance. So it seems like a bug but necessary. Ironic; isn't? Competition in-spite its benefits are because everybody is revolving within the same market with similar products and conditions; while bleats constantly remain insatiable and unchanging. Our market becomes more bubbling when it comes to this stage, energy of different statues, intent, directions and forces regularly exerting, all pushing the singular transaction goal.

How about cracking through a fallow ground, or re-branding a product, re-packaging a service profile [I give this suggestion when you have goofed, badly]? This distinguishes you in crawling world; when you serve saturation; praxis of trading becomes eminent. Your line of business must remain monopoly, and if your package is better enough then push it to the lode, and then make the lode your trademark [™]. When you give attention to events and conditions, you are definitely going to lose the way. The business' clan remains a business, organizational hutch.

This rule is commonly exercised though, but often time not well strategize to invade the public, it comes like a flint and off it goes. One of the ways to scatter market gaze is to launch at odd times, when no one is convinced enough to be in the market [this seems to be one of warren's secrets.

And, this is also one of the principles of market leaders – *effective executive meeting(s) is never done when market is on.* So leaders; the lesson is this: delegate when no one can alter, they create the conditions, and stipulate it.

When this is done, when you have done the odd plans and decisions, to get market focus, attract its attention with what is enough to pull its attention. Hope, survival, and satisfaction, confidence, reality, sacrifice [for their sake] and future: these are things market look out for. Create them, and bash out into the sky, after you it runs.

RULE # 10

SAVE TIME
–PROGRAM TIME AND DON'T ALLOW TIME PROGRAM YOU

"Time utility and maximization is the last, and what I want to tell you about this is simple. Plan and project with time; it pays. Don't allow your time program to ever fail. When your time fails, it means time programmed you" says the last business' clan chief I spoke with almost at the verge of stopping. I was tired of writing because they said everything, even things I presumed business are up to.

Most people have no real time; they plan time but don't work by it. It is the worst state to be –when time programs you. It has you. When this happens, the best you can have is nothing, at least never what you really need nor wished to have, but what time has for you.

All we have studied are both things I was told: rules, story, and lessons, applicable during my adventure to business' clan. Included also, are analyses

CHAPTER SUMMARY

- Every rule has its attitude

- To get the best of a rule understand its attitude and applicable environment

- Business rule is a standard. None is an opinion. It is the whole rule that builds up the negotiator we are talking about.

- The rules are in summaries list:

Rule No. 1: The Law of Necessity

Rule No. 2: Don't Outrun the Policy

Rule No. 3: Learn to be in Control

Rule No. 4: The Rule of Activities

Rule No. 5: Cost your Spills

Rule No. 6: Be Natural

Rule No. 7: The Intelligent Weakness

Rule No. 8: Emotion-ability

Rule No. 9: Praxis of Branding

Rule No. 10: Save Time